# SpringerBriefs in Law

More information about this series at http://www.springer.com/series/10164

Marco Casagrande

# Seaports in International Law

Springer

Marco Casagrande
Rome
Italy

ISSN 2192-855X ISSN 2192-8568 (electronic)
SpringerBriefs in Law
ISBN 978-3-319-60395-7 ISBN 978-3-319-60396-4 (eBook)
DOI 10.1007/978-3-319-60396-4

Library of Congress Control Number: 2017945710



Printed on acid-free paper

This Springer imprint is published by Springer Nature
The registered company is Springer International Publishing AG
The registered company address is: Gewerbestrasse 11, 6330 Cham, Switzerland

# Contents

# Part I
# Introduction

# Chapter 1
# The Lack of Interest for Seaports in the International Law and Doctrine

Even the greatest naval and maritime Superpowers in history are seldom associated with their ports. The still visible London Docks are a symbol of the British Empire, but much less than the Red Coats, the Royal Navy or British India. This mist of oblivion surrounding seaports is even more thick in the case of Venice. The Arsenal, the State shipyard which is considered the first assembly line facility in the world, is still a reminder of the might of the Most Serene Republic, but few people even know where the main port of Venice was (on Lido-San Nicolò).

Under this respect, the world of international law looks quite similar to the universe of popular culture. In the United Nations Cumulative Indexes, which include all the international agreements registered with the United Nations and the Secretariat of the League of Nations, only 306 instruments are classified as having as their subject "Ports".

However, in the whole list you will find only a single major multilateral treaty regulating ports, id est the 1923 Geneva Convention.[1] The vast majority of the other treaties can be divided into two categories. To the first category belong the loan agreements and guarantee agreements stipulated by States (usually developing States) and international financial Institutions such as the World Bank in order to finance the building, and the maintenance or the renovation of a seaport; such agreements contain standard financial clauses and are not very significant from the point of view of the legal regulation of seaports. The second category is very specific and includes the bilateral agreements made by the United States pursuant to the Deepwater Port Act[2]; these particular agreements will be examined in due course.[3]

---

[1]League of Nations (1926–1927).
[2]U.S. House of Representatives (2017), Title 33, Chap. 29.
[3]See Chap. 11.



M. Casagrande, *Seaports in International Law*, SpringerBriefs in Law,
DOI 10.1007/978-3-319-60396-4_1

Once you have excluded these two kinds of treaties, beside the aforementioned Geneva Convention just 19 international agreements will remain, including two for which no text is available.[4] Between these 19 treaties, most regulate the sea lanes served by the ports involved[5] or the rights and obligations of the ships using the said ports.[6] In the end, the international agreements regulating some aspects of port administration, port management or port operations, including port inspections not exclusively related to ship standards, are just six: a bilateral agreement on frontier controls between Great Britain and France,[7] a cooperation agreement applying to the Port Authorities of Strasbourg and Kehl,[8] two ILO Conventions,[9] the Convention of Mar del Plata[10] and an agreement between France and Monaco on the appointment of the Director of the Port of Monaco.[11]

The jurisprudence of international Courts, including WTO quasi-judicial bodies,[12] presents very few cases involving seaports; or rather, as it will be seen further on, has some landmark cases in which the port aspects, while present, were completely overlooked.[13]

As for the legal doctrine, in the Catalogue of the Peace Palace Library 258 books are classified under the subject "Ports", but only 19 of these treat harbors as a specific and unitary topic.[14] In all the other cases, the port is analyzed within treatises of maritime law or coastal law (especially national administrative law applying to coastal assets), or which are focused on a very specific port issue (typically dock work, Port State Control or competition law as applied to port infrastructures).

The picture of EU law is more mixed. The European Court of Justice has issued a landmark competition law judgment in the port of Genoa case,[15] leading to a

---

[4]Only the registration certificate was retrieved for the following treaties: United Nations (1994, 1996).

[5]United Nations (1957, 2005, 2007).

[6]Department of Foreign Affairs and Trade (1988) and United Nations (1948, 1960, 1964, 1982, 1998, 2003).

[7]United Nations (2004).

[8]United Nations (1995).

[9]International Labour Organization (2016) and United Nations (1975). See also paragraph 3 of this chapter, in which further ILO Conventions are mentioned; however, those Conventions mostly lay down technical specifics about port structures and do not impact significantly on port management.

[10]United Nations (1986).

[11]United Nations (1976).

[12]See Chap. 17.

[13]See Chap. 8.

[14]Burns (2015), Gutierrez Herran (2012), Maresca (2012), Hass-Engel (2009), Talley (2009), Alderton (2008), Carbone and Munari (2006), Van Hooydonk (2003), Chlomoudis (2002), Maresca (2001), Douglas (1983), Douglas (1989), En Sai (1918), Regul (1971), Tatangelo (1969), Abent (1944), Pagès (1938), Vaes (1904), and Quinette de Rochemont (1891). The list includes books on the colonial "treaty ports" (see Chap. 5), which were port cities rather than harbors.

[15]European Court of Justice (1991).

comprehensive if still incomplete reform of port legislation in Italy.[16] After that, however, the European Parliament rejected the so-called "Port Package I"[17] proposed by the European Commission, which afterwards abandoned also the plan to present a softer "Port Package II".[18] Similarly, the announced Commission Guidelines on State aids in the port sector[19] were never adopted. As it will be seen further on,[20] the abandonment of these legislative or quasi-legislative initiatives by the European Commission was not the consequence of a generic lack of consensus within the European Parliament or elsewhere, but of strong lobbying by the main actors of the old governance of seaports, id est the governance which has often been in place since before the containerization.

These actors are still deeply rooted in many port clusters, and it is impossible to predict if and when the EU law will retake the vanguard role it briefly had in the regulation of seaports.

Hopefully, this will happen sooner or later, perhaps starting with the adoption of the third Ports Package adopted by the Commission, this time in the form of a Draft Regulation.[21]

## References

Abent, H. (1944). *Treaty ports*. Garden City: Dubleday, Doran & Company.

Alderton, P. (2008). *Port management and operations*. London: Informa.

Burns, M. (2015). *Port management and operations*. Boca Raton: CRC Press, Taylor & Francis Group.

Carbone, S., & Munari, F. (2006). *La disciplina dei porti tra diritto comunitario e diritto interno*. Milan: Giuffrè.

Chlomoudis, C., & Pallis, A. (2002). *European Union port policy*. Chaltenham: Elgar.

Council of the European Union. (2014). *Proposal for a regulation of the European Parliament and of the council establishing a framework on market access to port services and financial transparency of ports (first reading)*. Interinstitutional File: 2013/0157 (COD).

Department of Foreign Affairs and Trade. (1988). Exchange of letters constituting an agreement between the Government of Australia and the Government of the United States of America concerning the access to repairs and maintenance facilities of Australian ports by United States Fishing vessels fishing in waters outside the Australian fishing zone, Port Moresby, 2 April 1987. *Australian Treaty Series*, p. 44.

Douglas, R. P. A. (1983). *An outline of the law relating to harbours in great britain managed under statutory powers* (II ed.). London: Lloyd's of London Press.

Douglas, R. P. A., & Geen, G. K. (1989). *The law of harbours and pilotage*. London: Lloyd's of London Press.

[16]State Printing Service and Mint (1994).

[17]European Commission (2002).

[18]European Commission (2004).

[19]European Parliament (2008), n. 8.

[20]Under Chap. 13.

[21]In its latest version: Council of the European Union (2014).

En Sai, T. (1918). *Treaty ports in China*. New York: Columbia University.
European Commission. (2002). *Amended proposal for a Directive of the European Parliament and of the Council On Market Access to Port Services (Presented by the Commission pursuant to Article 250(2) of the EC Treaty).* * COM/2002/0101 final - COD 2001/0047 *.
European Commission. (2004). *Proposal for a Directive of the European Parliament and of the Council on Market Access to Port Services*, /* COM/2004/0654 final - COD 2004/0240 */.
European Court of Justice. (1991). Judgment of the Court of 10 December 1991, Merci convenzionali porto di Genova SpA v Siderurgica Gabrielli SPA, Case C-179/90. *European Court Reports*, p. I-05889.
European Parliament. (2008). *Resolution of 4 September 2008 on a European ports policy* (2008/2007(INI)).
Gutierrez Herran, O. (2012). *Derecho portuario colombiano*. Bogotá: Pontificia Universidad Javeriana-Grupo Editorial Ibáñez-CEFIDES.
Hass-Engel, R. (2009). *The 2008 Indonesian Shipping Act and related aspects*. Maastricht: Legal Advisory Agency Indonesia.
International Labour Organization. (2016). C163 - Seafarers' Welfare Convention, 1987 (No. 163), *ILO*. https://www.ilo.org/dyn/normlex/en/f?p=NORMLEXPUB:12100:0::NO::P12100_INSTRUMENT_ID:312308
League of Nations. (1926–1927). Convention and Statute on the International Régime of Maritime Ports, Geneva, 9 December 1923. *League of Nations Treaty Series* (Vol. 58, p. 285).
Maresca, M. (2001). *La regolazione dei porti fra diritto interno e diritto comunitario*. Turin: Giappichelli.
Maresca, D. (2012). *La disciplina giuridica delle infrastrutture portuali: assetti istituzionali e regolazione del mercato tra diritto interno e diritto dell'Unione Europea*. Turin: Giappichelli.
Pagès, X. (1938). *L'administration des ports en France*. Paris: Recueil Sirey.
Quinette de Rochemont, D. (1891). *Les ports allemand de la Baltique*. Paris: Dunod.
Regul, R., & Anselin, M. (1971). *L'avenir des ports européens*. Bruges: De Tempel.
State Printing Service and Mint. (1994). Legge 29 gennaio 1994, n. 84. *Gazzetta Ufficiale della Repubblica Italiana*, n. 28 of 4 February 1994.
Talley, W. (2009). *Port economics*. Abingdon: Routledge.
Tatangelo, G. (1969). *I porti marittimi italiani*. Milan: Giuffrè.
United Nations. (1948). Reciprocal trade agreement between the United States of America and Mexico, Washington, 23 December 1942. In *United Nations Treaty Series* (Vol. 13, p. 231).
United Nations. (1957). Agreement between Italy and Austria concerning the use of the Port of Trieste, Rome, 22 October 1955. In *United Nations Treaty Series* (Vol. 260, p. 327).
United Nations. (1960). Exchange of notes constituting and agreement concerning reciprocal exemption from the measurement of ships in Port, Caracas, 20 July 1956. In *United Nations Treaty Series* (Vol. 351, p. 289).
United Nations. (1964). Agreement between the Government of the United States of America and the Government of the Kingdom of Belgium on the Visit of the N/S Savannah to Belgian Ports, Brussels, 19 April 1963. In *United Nations Treaty Series* (Vol. 493, p. 83).
United Nations. (1975). Convention (No. 137) Concerning the Social Repercussions of New Methods of Cargo Handling in Docks, Geneva, 25 June 1973. In *United Nations Treaty Series* (Vol. 976, p. 343).
United Nations. (1976). Exchange of letters constituting an agreement on methods of recruitment of the Director of the Port of Monaco, Monaco, 7 May 1973. In *United Nations Treaty Series* (Vol. 981, p. 271).
United Nations. (1982). Treaty on Pacific Coast Albacore Tuna Vessels and Port Privileges, Washington, 26 May 1981. In *United Nations Treaty Series* (Vol. 1274, p. 247).
United Nations. (1986). Inter-American Convention on Facilitation of International Waterborne Transportation, Mar del Plata, 7 June 1963. In *United Nations Treaty Series* (Vol. 1438, p. 172).
United Nations. (1994). Umbrella Agreement, New York, 25 August 1994. In *United Nations Treaty Series* (Vol. 1820, p. 461).

United Nations. (1995). Agreement concerning cooperation between the port authorities of Strasbourg and Kehl, Strasbourg, 23 September 1992. In *United Nations Treaty Series* (Vol. 1858, p. 381).

United Nations. (1996). Agreement on financial cooperation for the project "Technical, Economic and Environmental Studies for the Improvement of Traffic of Goods and Persons within the Corridor Rio de Janeiro-Sao Paulo-Campinas, including access to the ports of the region, Brasilia, 6 April 1995". In *United Nations Treaty Series* (Vol. 1905, p. 267).

United Nations. (1998). Agreement concerning specific stability requirements for Ro-Ro passenger ships undertaking regular scheduled international voyages between or to or from designated ports in North West Europe and the Baltic Sea, Stockholm, 27–28 February 1996. In *United Nations Treaty Series* (Vol. 2010, p. 175).

United Nations. (2003). Agreement between the United States of America and Poland relating to port access procedures, Warsaw, 20 April-31 May 1990. In *United Nations Treaty Series* (Vol. 2207, p. 193).

United Nations. (2004). Treaty between the Government of the United Kingdom of Great Britain and Northern Ireland and the Government of the French Republic concerning the implementation of frontier controls at the sea ports of both countries on the Channel and North Sea, Le Touquet, 4 February 2003. In *United Nations Treaty Series* (Vol. 2290, p. 159).

United Nations. (2005). Agreement between the Government of the Republic of Lithuania and the Government of the Republic of Uzbekistan on transport and transport related services rendered to the Freight of Uzbekistan in transit through the Klaipėda State Seaport, Tashkent, 20 February 1997. In *United Nations Treaty Series* (Vol. 2334, p. 21).

United Nations. (2007). Agreement between the Government of the Republic of Lithuania and the Government of the Republic of Kazakhstan on transport and transport related services rendered to the freight of Kazakhstan in transit through the Klaipeda State Seaport, Almaty, 7 March 1997. In *United Nations Treaty Series* (Vol. 2412, p. 41).

U.S. House of Representatives. (2017). *United States Code.* http://uscode.house.gov/

Vaes, G. (1904). *Les ports belges.* Brussels: Larcier, Bruxelles.

Van Hooydonk, E. (2003). *European seaports law.* Antwerp: Maklu.

# Chapter 2
# The Port and the International Law in General: A Land Appendix

The lack of interest shown for seaports by the international legal order can be partly explained by the interference of the principle of domestic jurisdiction.[1] Indeed, civilian seaports used to be a national asset, under the full sovereignty and administration of the port State, and with their management strongly (and jealously) dominated by local organizations and entities.[2] Therefore, any form of international regulation appeared unnecessary, and was not even considered by the international community.

The condition of military seaports (naval bases) was completely different, since it was not unusual for strategic naval bases to be under the control of a foreign Power different than the port State. In this case, in order to safeguard the sovereignty of the territorial State, the granting of a naval base has been based on international agreements analytically regulating the relationship between the territorial State and the Power of the naval base.

However, even the provisions of the international agreements applying to foreign naval bases fail to specifically focus on seaports. In most cases, the granting of the naval bases is treated merely as a granting of territory, clearly because territory is perceived as a constitutive element of the State, thus making any granting of international rights to a foreign Power over it a particularly sensitive issue. This will usually lead the contracting Powers to neglect the water and port component of the naval base involved.

The provisions of the treaty of Utrecht,[3] regulating the transfer of Gibraltar from Spain to Great Britain, treat what was clearly a naval base under every respect—strategical, geopolitical and practical—as a "town and castle": "La ciudad y castillo de Gibraltar, juntamente con su puerto, defensas y fortaleza que le pertecenen" in the Spanish text; "the town and castle of Gibraltar, together with the port, fortifi-

[1]The question of whether domestic jurisdiction should be considered a principle of law, a general provision of the international legal order or otherwise classified will be left open here.
[2]See Chap. 6.
[3]Baskett (1714).



M. Casagrande, *Seaports in International Law*, SpringerBriefs in Law,
DOI 10.1007/978-3-319-60396-4_2

cations, and forts thereunto belonging" in the English text; "proprietatem urbis et arcis Gibraltar noncupatae, una cum portu, munitionibus, fortalitiis eodemque pertinentibus" in the Latin text.[4] The port is indeed mentioned, but just as an accessory of the fortress town. It is therefore no surprise that, as part of the ongoing controversy between Great Britain and Spain on the status of Gibraltar, both parties agree that the Utrecht Treaty cannot be considered a sufficient basis for Britain to claim any sovereign right over the territorial waters of Gibraltar.[5] Since the Rock is clearly a naval outpost to control the access to the Strait of the same name, the drafting of the norm is quite staggering; and yet, this is far from being an isolated case.

Another important element of British international practice is the 1921 Anglo-Irish Treaty, by which the United Kingdom,[6] in granting independence to Ireland, reserved to itself, among other things, the control over some strategical naval bases, the so-called "treaty ports". Also in this case, no mention at all is made of the British sovereign rights over the Irish waters served by the said ports, which are referred as "such harbour and other facilities as are indicated in the Annex hereto, or such other facilities as may from time to time be agreed between the British Government and the Government of the Irish Free State."[7] The only mention of water or underwater facilities (submarine cables and navigation signals) is found in the Annex to the Treaty, and apparently the British Government was content with leaving the control of those facilities to Ireland, subject to its supervision. Yet, just like in the case of Gibraltar, it is obvious that Britain, by putting the treaty into execution, acquired extensive sovereign rights over the Irish waters, so much that, when the controversial concession of the treaty ports was revoked, the Irish Minister of Foreign Affairs told the Irish Parliament that new agreement with Britain would reinstate "Irish sovereignty over the Twenty-Six Counties and the territorial sea."[8]

Finally, a relevant element of British practice is the agreement with the United States on the use by the latter of some islands of the British Indian Ocean Territory, in particular the Diego Garcia atoll, which hosts an important US naval base. The agreement,[9] dating back to the Sixties, again does not explicitly regulate the legal

---

[4]Artículo X in the Spanish text, Article X in the English text, Articulus X in the Latin text.

[5]United Nations (2013). See Spanish declaration upon signature (December 4, 1984): "The Spanish Government, upon signing this Convention, declares that this act cannot be interpreted as recognition of any rights or situations relating to the maritime spaces of Gibraltar which are not included in article 10 of the Treaty of Utrecht of 13 July 1713 between the Spanish and British Crowns". An identical declaration was made my Spain upon ratification (January 15, 1997). The United Kingdom itself bases its claim on the continued and undisputed control of the water rather than on the treaty, an argument which is equally rejected by Spain: Gobierno de España (2017).

[6]The National Archives of Ireland (1998).

[7]Art. 7.

[8]Oireachtas (1938).

[9]United Nations (1967).

status of the island waters; in 1972, via a supplementary agreement,[10] the United Kingdom assumed the obligation to forbid commercial fishing in the internal and external waters of Diego Garcia, including the Exclusive Economic Zone.[11] After that, further supplementary agreements gave to the United States extensive rights of jurisdiction over the Diego Garcia waters.[12]

In the Diego Garcia example it can be noticed that the United States practice, in comparison to the British one, appears to be more inclined to an explicit regulation of the status of the waters surrounding its overseas naval bases. Indeed, also the 1903 agreement between the United States and Cuba on the lease of the Guantanamo Bay naval base[13] contained a very clear provision: "The grant of the foregoing Article shall include the right to use and occupy the waters adjacent to said areas of land and water."[14]

However, after World War II, when the United States developed their "imperial" network of overseas military bases, the water component of the military bases started again to fade, or rather the naval bases ceased to be distinguished from the land and air bases, no matter how great their strategical significance. All the US military installations covered by the agreement with a given host country have simply been regulated in the same way.

Since the United States maintains hundreds of military installations in different foreign countries, it is impossible to examine all the relevant agreements. However, it is possible to limit the research to the major US overseas naval bases. Only three countries host US naval bases which are a Fleet HQ: Italy (HQ of the Sixth Fleet in Naples), Bahrain (HQ of the Fifth Fleet in Manama), and Japan (HQ of the Seventh Fleet in Yokosuka).

Italy and the United States are both parts of the NATO Status of Forces Agreement,[15] but the United States has also concluded bilateral agreements with the individual NATO members hosting their bases. Italy and the United States concluded in 1954 a Bilateral Infrastructure Agreement (BIA), also known as "Umbrella Agreement", which is however classified.[16]

The 1971 agreement between Bahrain and the United States is highly atypical.[17] On a first look, it appears an agreement regulating the transitional permanence of an expeditionary corps on foreign soil rather than the long-term establishment of military bases, and indeed it does not make any mention of military installations except for "support facilities" whose regime is to be established by "administrative

[10]United Nations (1973).

[11]Art. 12.

[12]United Nations (1976), par. 8.c, on recreational fishing by the British personnel stationed on the island; United Nations (1998), par. 5, on dredging operations and environmental protection.

[13]Skylar and Hagen (1972).

[14]Art. II.

[15]United Nations (1954).

[16]Ronzitti (2007), p. 4.

[17]United Nations (1972).

arrangements between the United States authorities and the authorities of Bahrain or, as appropriate, private property owners."[18] However, the agreement is more or less explicitly stipulated for an indefinite duration,[19] and the United States still maintains a strong presence in Bahrain. The ambiguous wording of the agreement is probably an attempt not to hurt too much the sensitivities of the Muslim population in Bahrain and in the neighboring States, which has traditionally been hostile to the presence of Western troops on Arabian soil; under this respect, the presence of a foreign force is probably more palatable than permanent foreign bases. In any case, what is relevant for this treatise is that also the Bahrein agreement puts on the same footing the land, sea, and air units of the United States, thus lacking any specific regulation of the naval bases even under the guise of "naval support structures," "ports of call used by the U.S. Navy," or similar expressions.

Finally, the agreement between the United States and Japan applies an identical legal regime to the U.S. land, naval, and air bases.[20]

In conclusion, the norms of international treaty law applying to overseas naval bases will focus on the terrestrial component of the said bases, without putting a particular emphasis on their naval character or their unavoidable influence over the territorial waters of the host States. This approach must probably be attributed to the sensitivity of stationing foreign troops on the soil of a State, thus directly affecting its territory, which is often—albeit not always—considered as a constitutive element of the State as an international subject. The mere presence of foreign military ships in the territorial waters, even if permanent, is considered less problematic,[21] and the attention of the negotiators remains monopolized by the necessity of safeguarding, with explicit and possibly analytical norms, the territorial integrity of the host State.

Even when the waters serving the naval base are mentioned and regulated, they are treated as an accessory to the land component of the base.[22]

As it will be seen further on, this approach can be detected even in the international regulation of the colonial factories, the peculiar overseas ports/outposts/naval bases which in the era of the so-called "informal colonial empires" were the cornerstone of European colonial policy.[23]

---

[18]Art. 13.

[19]Art. 14: "Should either government determine at some future time that it is no longer desirable to continue the presence on Bahrain of the United States Middle East Force, the United States shall have one year thereafter to terminate its presence".

[20]United Nations (1960).

[21]Significantly, the Montego Bay Convention allows the innocent passage of foreign military vessels in the territorial waters of a State: United Nations (1994), art. 17–26. See also International Court of Justice (1949).

[22]The understanding of the waters served by a naval base as a mere accessory to the base appears to have influenced also the international practice related to domestic naval bases. Some States have declared the territorial waters served by a naval base special military areas which are permanently closed to the innocent passage of foreign ships, even if it is dubious whether the international law of the sea allows such a permanent limitation: see Ridolfi (1997).

[23]See Chap. 5.

The only seaports which can rival the old factories in terms of economical and strategical significance—albeit not mirroring the military importance of the former—are today's multimodal ports, key hubs of the container shipping industry, which is considered the conveyor belt of globalization. Given these premises, one would expect international commercial law to have drastically increased the amount of consideration given to the regulation of seaports. However, this is not the case, as it will be seen further on.[24]

## References


Baskett, printer. (1714). *Tractatus pacis & amicitiae inter serenissimam ac potentissimam principem Annam... et serenissiman ac potentissimam principem Philippum V ... concluses Trajecti ad Rhenum die 2/13 mensis julii, anno 1713. Treaty of peace and friendship between... Anne, by grace of God, queen of Great Britain, France, and Ireland... and Philip the Vth, the Catholik king of Spain, concluded at Utrecht the 2/13 day of July, 1713.* London: Baskett (by Her Majesties Special Command).

Gobierno de España. (2017). Historia y aspectos Jurídicos del contencioso. *Gobierno de España.* http://www.exteriores.gob.es/Portal/es/PoliticaExteriorCooperacion/Gibraltar/Paginas/Historia.aspx

International Court of Justice. (1949). Corfu Channel case, Judgment of April 9th, 1949. *I.C.J. Reports*, p. 4.

Oireachtas. (1938). *Diospoireachtai Parlaiminte*, Volume 71, sitting of 27 April 1938.

Ridolfi, G. (1997). Geostrategy and naval power in the Mediterranean. *Marine Policy, 21*(4), 387.

Ronzitti, N. (Ed.). (2007). *Le basi americane in Italia - problemi aperti.* Rome: Senato della Repubblica.

Skylar, B., & Hagen, V. M., compilers. (1972). Agreement between the United States and Cuba for the lease of lands for coaling and naval stations, Havana-Washington, 16 February 1903–23 February 1903. *Inter-American Relations.* Washington, D.C.: U.S. Government Printing Office.

The National Archives of Ireland. (1998). *Final text of the Articles of Agreement for a Treaty between Great Britain and Ireland as signed.* NAI DE 2/304/1, n. 214.

United Nations. (1954). Agreement between the Parties to the North Atlantic Treaty regarding the status of their forces, London, 19 June 1951. In *United Nations Treaty Series* (Vol. 199, p. 67).

United Nations. (1960). Agreement under article VI of the Treaty of mutual cooperation between Japan and the United States of America, regarding facilities and areas and the status of the United States armed forces in Japan. In *United Nations Treaty Series* (Vol. 373, p. 179).

United Nations. (1967). Availability of certain Indian Ocean islands for defence purposes: Agreement effected by exchange of notes. In *United Nations Treaty Series* (Vol. 603, p. 273).

United Nations. (1972). Exchange of notes constituting an agreement to maintain deployment in Bahrain of the United States Middle East Force, including its flagship and other vessels and aircraft, Manama, 23 December 1971. In *United Nations Treaty Series* (Vol. 823, p. 157).

United Nations. (1973). Naval communications facility on Diego Garcia. In *United Nations Treaty Series* (Vol. 866, p. 302).

United Nations. (1976). Supplementary arrangements 1976: Naval support facility on Diego Garcia—agreement effected by exchange of notes. In *United Nations Treaty Series* (Vol. 1018, p. 372).


[24]See Chap. 17.

United Nations. (1994). United Nations convention on the law of the sea, Montego Bay, 10 December 1982. In *United Nations Treaty Series* (Vol. 1833, p. 396).

United Nations. (1998). Supplemental arrangements of 1982 relating to the facility of Diego Garcia. In *United Nations Treaty Series* (Vol. 2001, p. 397).

United Nations. (2013). Declarations and statements. *United Nations.* http://www.un.org/Depts/los/convention_agreements/convention_declarations.htm

# Chapter 3
# The Port and the Law of the Sea: An Accessory to the Waters

In the framework of a general lack of consideration for port issues in the international legal order, the law of the sea could be expected to have a spearhead role in framing a regulation of harbors.

However, the Montego Bay Convention,[1] by far the main international instrument codifying and innovating the law of the sea, mentions seaports only in 16 articles in 320, and principally for the purposes of maritime delimitation, as it will be seen further on.[2]

Under this respect, the approach of the Montego Bay Convention can be considered illustrative of that which is adopted by those branches of international law which have traditionally regulated some aspect of maritime affairs, for example international labor law.[3] Within the ILO standards, as many as 36 Conventions were adopted to regulate seafaring since 1920, so much that in 2006 the Maritime

---

[1]United Nations (1994).

[2]Under Chap. 11.

[3]The particular focus of international labor law on maritime affairs is due to the peculiar features of seafaring. Seafarers will often work on the high seas, and the legal discipline of their work, in order to be effective, must be to some degree internationalized or at least harmonized at the international level. It is no accident that seafarers are organized in long-established and particularly active international trade unions, the most important one being probably the International Transport Workers' Federation. The need for an international regulation and protection of seafarers has been made even more compelling by the weakening of the jurisdictional link between flag States and ships (see Chap. 14).



M. Casagrande, *Seaports in International Law*, SpringerBriefs in Law,
DOI 10.1007/978-3-319-60396-4_3

Labour Convention was adopted as some sort of codification. In contrast, only four Conventions were adopted to regulate dock work.[4]

The relationship between seafaring and dock work within international labor law mirrors the relationship between the water component and the land component of the port in the law of the sea: the former is the focus of the legal regulation, while the latter is an accessory to the waters (and the ships) served by the harbor.

This approach only apparently contradicts the outline in the previous chapter with reference to other branches of international law less directly involved with ports. Indeed, the lack of interest in the land component of ports showed by the international law of the sea is nothing else that a different expression of the constant concern of international law with the protection of State sovereignty. As seen above, the main sources of international law applying to seaports—outside of the law of the seas and other legal branches more strictly connected with seaports—are the international agreements regulating overseas naval bases.

In the case of a naval base, the main interference with the sovereignty of the host State comes from the land component of the port, overshadowing even the very legitimate concerns which could arouse from the stationing in the port of major warships, for example a U.S. nuclear-powered aircraft carrier.[5]

Instead, in the case of civilian seaports, to which the law of the seas mostly applies, the main interference with the sovereignty of the port State comes from foreign ships using the port. After all, a ship is an organized community, at least partially regulated by a foreign legal order (the law of the flag) and subject to an internal hierarchy headed by an organ of a foreign State with wide-ranging powers (the master).[6] This was particularly true some decades ago, when the link between the ship and the flag State was more effective and the crews were mostly made by citizens of the flag State enrolled in its merchant navy. Moreover, due to the lack of a quick line of communication between the flag State and its ships abroad, the

---

[4]International Labour Organization (2016a, b); United Nations (1975, 1982). The first Convention, dating back to 1929, is no more in force. It had been originally ratified by Ireland, Luxembourg, Nicaragua, and Spain. However, Ireland and Spain subsequently ratified the revised Convention. Pursuant to Article 23, paragraph 1 of the 1929 Convention, "Should the Conference adopt a new Convention revising this Convention in whole or in part, the ratification by a Member of the new revising Convention shall ipso jure involve denunciation of this Convention without any requirement of delay, notwithstanding the provisions of Article 21 above, if and when the new revising Convention shall have come into force". The third paragraph of the same Article reads "Nevertheless, this Convention shall remain in force in its actual form and content for those Members which have ratified it but have not ratified the revising Convention". After Luxembourg denounced the 1929 Convention pursuant to its Article 21, Nicaragua remained the only contracting Party: International Labour Organization (2016c). According the ILO ratification table, the Convention is still in force for Ecuador; however, it is dubious if an international treaty can be considered as being in force for only one international subject.

[5]In the end warships, despite still needing land bases, project their strategic influence on the seas they patrol and on the respective coastal States, rather than on the (usually friendly) State hosting their logistical base.

[6]Quadri (1939), p. 32.

powers of the commander (and of the consular representatives of the flag State in foreign ports)[7] were remarkable. Significantly, foreign ships used to be sometimes considered a portion of the territory of the flag State (territoire flottant).[8]

This emphasis on the status of foreign ships using the port and consequently on the sea lanes and waters served by its installations left the international law without an organic regulation of harbors as organized systems of land installations, water installations, and waters devoted to the reception, loading, unloading, refueling, and assistance to ships. So much that, when in 2001 the so-called "War on Terror" required the quick enactment of new rules for port and container security, the international community found itself without any legal instrument to do so and—in order to avoid negotiating an entirely new treaty—was forced to bind the rules on amending procedures established in the International Convention for the Safety of Life at Sea.[9]

On the other hand, this approach did not even fulfill its purpose of safeguarding the sovereignty of the port State. Indeed, due to its focus on the status of ships, it was influenced by the relevant international practice, based on a very strong defense of the sovereign prerogatives of the flag State. The result was a legal regulation of seaports formally affirming the full jurisdiction of the port State over foreign ships calling at its ports, but only for facts occurred within the territorial waters of the port State, and even then contradicted by a constant, well-established practice of non-interference by the port State in the affairs of foreign ships. A practice so strong, and so intertwined with the usages of the maritime community, that it has made difficult the establishment of effective international Port State Control regimes.[10]

This legal framework, combined with the dogma of "port specificity" adopted and strenuously defended by many established port clusters, has left harbors in a limbo which is no more sustainable, given their essential role in the globalization and in the maintenance of international security.

## References

Anonymous. (1920–1921). Changes in the organization of the Foreign and Diplomatic Service. In *The British yearbook of international law* (p. 103).

International Labour Organization. (2016a). C028: Protection against Accidents (Dockers) Convention, 1929 (No. 28). *ILO*. http://www.ilo.org/dyn/normlex/en/f?p=NORMLEXPUB:12100:0::NO:12100:P12100_INSTRUMENT_ID:312173:NO

[7]In the past, the assistance to ships flying the flag of a State in foreign ports was considered the main task of the consular network of that State, as reported by Anonymous (1920–1921). It should be noted, however, that the anonymous author was describing the British Consular Service, which for clear historical reasons was likely to be particularly attentive to shipping affairs.

[8]Pugliatti (2011), Vol. IV, p. 564; see also Chap. 8.

[9]See Chap. 15.

[10]See Chap. 14.

International Labour Organization. (2016b). C032: Protection against Accidents (Dockers) Convention (Revised), 1932 (No. 32). *ILO*. http://www.ilo.org/dyn/normlex/en/f?p=NORMLEXPUB:12100:0::NO:12100:P12100_INSTRUMENT_ID:312177:NO
International Labour Organization. (2016c). Raifications of C028). *ILO*. http://www.ilo.org/dyn/normlex/en/f?p=NORMLEXPUB:11300:0::NO::P11300_INSTRUMENT_ID:312173
United Nations. (1975). Convention (No. 137) concerning the social repercussions of new methods of cargo handling in docks, Geneva, 25 June 1973. In *United Nations Treaty Series* (Vol. 976, p. 3).
United Nations. (1982). Convention (No. 152) concerning occupational safety and health in dock work, Geneva, 25 June 1979. In *United Nations Treaty Series* (Vol. 1260, p. 3).
United Nations. (1994). United Nations convention on the law of the Sea, Montego Bay, 10 December 1982. In *United Nations Treaty Series* (Vol. 1833, p. 396).
Pugliatti, S. (2011). *Scritti giuridici*. Milan: Giuffrè.
Quadri, R. (1939). *Le navi private nel diritto internazionale*. Milan: Giuffrè.

# Part II
# The Pre-industrial Port

# Chapter 4
# Paolo Sarpi's Legal Doctrine

The Most Serene Republic of Venice, the city-State which existed from the Middle Ages[1] until 1797, claimed sovereignty over the entire Adriatic Sea.[2]

One of the most illustrious Venetian legal scholars is the Servite friar Paolo Sarpi (1522–1623), whose statue can still be admired by the tourist in Campo Santa Fosca, along the Strada Nuova. In his work "Dominio del Mare Adriatico della Serenissima Repubblica di Venezia", which was written in support to the Venetian claim, Sarpi argues "It is an opinion universally held by the legal scholars that bays and ports (meaning the open bays and ports, since the enclosed ones will be discussed separately) are under the domination of the same subject which owns the sea, and specifically the Adriatic Sea. The experts confirming the dominion of the Most Serene Republic—and they explain that such dominion extends to bays and coves, which they call stations and ports—base such extension on the fact that those waters are contiguous with the sea waters, so that they cannot be demarcated and divided, and you cannot find a border between the port and the sea. Therefore they cannot be governed by two different subjects, but they will have the same status of the sea to which they belong, since there is no difference between deep water and low water—because you can also have, in some place near the land, a greater depth than far away. However, the formal reason for which all the sea water must be subject to the master of the sea is that the dominion of the sea ensures protection and safety to sailors and passengers; and bays, coves and ports are in greater need of such protection and defense, because there corsairs and maritime thieves can more easily execute their robberies: therefore the lord of the sea must keep and protect those place no less than the high seas—and even more, since the need is greater."[3]

---

[1]It is difficult to establish precisely the exact date in which Venice became an independent State, since the first Dogi ("Duces" in Latin) where officially Byzantine magistrates, even after they ceased to be appointed by the Emperor and were instead designated by the city itself.
[2]Daru (1832), p. 72.
[3]Sarpi (2001), pp. 78–79. Translation in English by the author.

 
M. Casagrande, *Seaports in International Law*, SpringerBriefs in Law,
DOI 10.1007/978-3-319-60396-4_4

Almost setting a legal pattern, Sarpi clearly and explicitly treats the seaports as a mere accessory to the sea. Indeed, his notion of seaport is limited to the waters of the seaport, so much that he prefers to call "bays and coves" what other law scholars call "stations and ports". The land facilities serving ports are considered irrelevant, despite the fact that Sarpi's Venice had in the Arsenale the most sophisticated naval base of its age.

Obviously, the significance of this passage by Sarpi should not be overstated. Not only his arguments were at least partly politically motivated, but as a scholar he operated within a completely different legal framework. Under the jus commune, between other things, the opinions of the most reputable law scholars were often considered a source of law in se. Moreover, the legal regime of the seas was an unexplored topic: after all, the international law did not exist yet.

Despite this, it is significant that Sarpi, between all the possible arguments put at his disposal by the jus commune—for example arguments based on jus naturale, aequitas, the argument of the impossibility to demark the waters, etc.—chose an approach which is already so similar to the one adopted after him, within completely different legal and factual frameworks.

## References

Daru, P.-A. (1832). *Storia della Repubblica di Venezia* (Vol. I). Capolago: Tipografia Elvetica.

Sarpi, P. (2001). *Dominio del Mare Adriatico della Serenissima Repubblica di Venezia*. Turin: Giappichelli.

# Chapter 5
# The Colonial Factories

After the so-called "Age of Discovery" (15 century), the task of exploring the newly discovered territories, trading with them and eventually colonizing them—formally or informally—was largely left by the European Governments to the private initiative of individuals and companies. Such individuals and companies exercised, de jure or de facto,[1] what are generally considered sovereign powers strictly reserved to the public Authorities of a State.

In order to fulfill their mission, the colonial enterprises established in the overseas territories outposts called "factories" ("feitorias" in Portuguese). Officially mere trading posts headed by a company official, the factories were usually naval bases built on the coast or up a river, protected by a garrison composed by foreign and locally recruited troops. Their establishment was the subject of an agreement between the colonial enterprise and the local Authorities, often in the form of a commercial contract rather than an international treaty. The agreement usually granted extensive public powers to the company official heading the trading post, who had full jurisdiction over the company employees, their families residing in the factory, the garrison guarding it, and the ships using the port.

Similar agreements were not regarded by the local Authorities as limitations to their territorial sovereignty, but rather as means to keep the foreign enclave completely separated by the local population, since they were—correctly—predicting

---

[1]The so-called "Chartered Companies", such as the famous Companies of the Indies established in various States, were usually explicitly granted sovereign powers by the legislation of their State of incorporation: for example the jus tractatus, the jus ad bellum, the power to raise armies and fleets, levy taxes, legislate over the overseas territories, etc. This was not always the case, however. The Rubattino Corporation, which purchased the first Italian footholds in the Horn of Africa, was a purely private corporation: Scovazzi (1996), p. 5ff. Similarly, sovereign powers were granted to individual explorers, colonizers, and administrators appointed under quasi-feudal rules, such as the English "proprietary governors". In many cases, however, the building of colonial Empires was partly accomplished by individuals acting purely in their private capacity, like Cecil Rhodes in Rhodesia or the Brooke dynasty in Sarawak.



M. Casagrande, *Seaports in International Law*, SpringerBriefs in Law,
DOI 10.1007/978-3-319-60396-4_5

that European encroachment would eventually destroy the existing political and social order.

An extreme example of these first-generation secluded factories is the one established by the Dutch East Indies Company in Deshima, Japan, in the 17 century. In that case, the Shogunate Government went so far in its isolation policy as to build in the Nagasaki Bay an artificial island which the Company employees, including their director (Opperhoofden), were strictly forbidden to leave.[2]

Since the local Authorities did not perceive the need to safeguard their territorial sovereignty—or at least believed that the best way to safeguard it was to isolate the foreign community so strictly that it was allowed to self-govern itself—the establishment of a factory was not the subject of an analytical legal regulation. This was also due to the uncertainty of the legal framework in which the negotiations between the colonial enterprises and the local Authorities took place. Was the agreement allowing the establishment of the factory an international agreement or a private law contract? Can an agreement with a Government devoid of any significant notion of international law as understood in Europe be considered an international treaty? If it was instead a private law contract, was it regulated by the municipal law of the local Authority or by the national law of the colonial enterprise? Moreover, the multiple roles held by the factories (trade post, government center, diplomatic–consular representation, military and naval base, etc.) did not allow for a proper consideration of their maritime role, even if in most cases a factory was a naval base the strategic value of which consisted in its ability to oversee a certain sea or sea passage (Tangier, the Cape, Aden, Singapore, etc.).

The trend of considering the factories a terrestrial outpost rather than a seaport was further strengthened by the gradual extension of the influence and control by the European powers over the territory surrounding the factories, which in time became the capitals of small colonial provinces; the said provinces, in turn, became the original nucleus of larger colonies or colonial federations.

The understanding of the factories as land territories rather than naval bases is clearly visible in the regulation by the classical and contemporary international law of some factories which, for different reasons, survived as such, rather than becoming included in larger colonial holdings: Tangier and the factories of Portuguese India.

Dating back to the Carthaginian Empire, Tangier was conquered by Portugal in 1471, thus becoming a factory headed by a Captain (Capitão). In 1661 the port city became an English factory with the unusual status of free city before being overrun by the local Sultan in 1684. Under ordinary circumstances, Tangier would have lost its role of factory forever, but the 19 century Scramble for Africa and the tensions which ultimately led to World War I led the European Powers to often overstate their differences, and the value of Tangier as a counterweight to British Gibraltar triggered a number of international crises involving Great Britain, France, and Germany.

---

[2]Gilbert (2006).

The Anglo-French victory in World War I was not enough to defuse the tensions, and in 1923 the city, while remaining under the nominal sovereignty of the Sultan of Morocco, was put under an international administration[3] acting under the control of Franco-British-Spanish Control Committee.

Even if the status of Tangier had always been a maritime power issue, the international regulation of the port city paid little attention to its maritime component. The only relevant provision is the one granting the powers of maritime policing jointly to the British, French, and Spanish Navies.[4] In contrast, the land policing of the city is much more analytically regulated, in order to balance the interests of the various foreign Powers, as well as the nominal sovereignty of the local Sultan. An ad hoc police corps was established, to be composed by Moroccans rank-and-file officers led by European commissioned and noncommissioned officers answering to the international administration.[5] The Moroccan subjects remained under the jurisdiction of the local Sultan,[6] while the European citizens would be tried by International Courts rather than by the customary consular Courts.[7] The city was demilitarized.[8] To sum it up, Tangier was treated as an international city similar to what was supposed to be the Free Territory of Trieste,[9] despite the fact

---

[3]Convention regarding the organization of the Statute of the Tangier Zone, in Stuart (1931), p. 239. In 1940 Spain unilaterally occupied the Tangier Zone, temporarily disbanding the international administration which was re-established in 1945: United Nations (1951). Spain lost the right to designate one of the three Administrators, the United States quota in the international Legislative Assembly was increased, and the Soviet Union was co-opted in the administration (United Nations 1951, Art. 7). Finally, in 1956 the city was returned to the newly independent Morocco: United Nations (1957).

[4]Art. 4 of the Convention.

[5]Art. 47 of the Convention. The international administration was in turn a very complicated balance between the interests held by several foreign Powers and by the local Sultan in Tangier. In the international Legislative Assembly four seats were allocated to Spain, four to France, three to the United Kingdom, two to Italy, one to the United States, one to Belgium, one to Portugal, one to the Netherlands, and nine to Morocco (three of the Moroccan seats were reserved to the local Jewish community). The administrator and his two deputies had to be citizens of different States.

[6]Art. 25 of the Convention.

[7]Art. 13 of the Convention.

[8]Art. 3 of the Convention.

[9]Pursuant to the Treaty of peace with Italy concluded after World War II (United Nations 1950), Trieste and its surrounding area should have become a Free Territory (art. 21, par. 1), not subject to Italian sovereignty (art. 21, par. 2), to be "governed in accordance with an instrument for a provisional regime drafted by the Council of Foreign Ministers and approved by the Security Council" until the entry into force of a Permanent Statute also approved by the Security Council (art. 21, par. 3). The beginning of the Cold War and the ensuing rift between the Soviet Union and the former Western Allies prevented the Security Council from approving the provisional regime, and the city remained subject to Anglo-American military administration until 1954, when Italy was able to reannex the city in exchange for the permanent cession to Yugoslavia of the former Italian territories East of Trieste: United Nations (1956). Before World War I, Trieste had been a strategic port of the Austro-Hungarian Empire, but its disputed status after World War II was mainly the result of the expansionist policies adopted by Tito's Yugoslavia against its former Italian enemy.

that its international status was undisputedly related to its position on the Atlantic Ocean, near the Strait of Gibraltar.

Even more typical factories were the tiny, predominantly coastal enclaves which, until 1961, were part of the Portuguese Estado da India. The Estado was what was left of the network of Portuguese feitorias established in India during the 14 century. Thereafter, the French and especially British expansion in India, coupled with the decline of the Portuguese Empire, caused these factories to maintain their original character of outposts, rather than becoming the capital or larger Portuguese colonial holdings like their African counterparts in Portuguese Guinea, Angola, and Mozambique.

After becoming independent in 1947, India started boycotting the Estado, notably denying Portugal the permit to move its police and troops to the inland enclaves in order to suppress the local movement pressing for annexation by India. As a result, some enclaves became de facto independent territories, and Portugal submitted an application instituting proceedings to the International Court of Justice,[10] the jurisdiction of which had been accepted by India.[11]

Portugal based its claim on a 1779 treaty with a Maratha ruler and local custom.[12] The Court found that the treaty did not transfer to Portugal the sovereignty over the inland enclaves, which had been acquired by Portugal only after the passage of India under British sovereignty.[13] The United Kingdom, according to the Court, had renounced any claim of sovereignty over the enclaves and let Portugal exercise "exclusive authority" over them.[14] The Court, however, recognized the existence of a local custom granting Portugal a right of passage, but only limited to "private persons, civil officials and goods in general" and excluding "armed forces, armed police and arms and ammunition".[15]

What is herein relevant is the fact that Portugal did not even attempt to base his claim on any law of the sea or transportation law norm, for example, the right to access to the sea.[16] Such an argument would have not been more far-fetched that invoking a local or special custom, the latter being difficult to prove, uncertain in its consensual or customary nature, and—in the end—unlikely to be recognized by the Court.[17]

[10]International Court of Justice (1955).

[11]International Court of Justice (1955), par. 22.

[12]International Court of Justice (1960), par. 21.

[13]International Court of Justice (1960), pp. 36–37.

[14]International Court of Justice (1960), p. 37.

[15]International Court of Justice (1960), p. 38ff.

[16]See Chap. 7.

[17]International Court of Justice (1952), p. 27ff., International Court of Justice (1950), p. 15ff., International Court of Justice (1951) recognized as a customary norm the peculiar "Norwegian system" of delimitation of the territorial sea, but it is a case of universal customary norm applying to Norway, rather than of local or special custom: see International Court of Justice (1951), p. 27.

Both the Tangier and the Estado da India case, therefore, confirm that, when seaports are considered under the lens of the general corpus of international law, their maritime characteristics tend to be completely forgotten.[18]

## References

Gilbert, M. J. (2006). Paper trails: Deshima island: A stepping stone between civilizations. In *World history connected.* http://worldhistoryconnected.press.illinois.edu/3.3/gilbert.html

International Court of Justice. (1950). Colombian-Peruvian asylum case, Judgment of November 20th, 1950. *I.C.J. Reports* (p. 266).

International Court of Justice. (1951). Fisheries case, Judgment of December 18th, 1951. *I.C. J. Reports* (p. 116).

International Court of Justice. (1952). Case concerning rights of nationals of the United States of America in Morocco. Judgment of August 27th, 1952. *I.C.J. Reports* (p. 176).

International Court of Justice. (1955). Application 22 XII 55. *I.C.J. Pleadings.* Case concerning right of passage over Indian territory (Vol. 1, p. 2).

International Court of Justice. (1960). Case concerning right of passage over Indian territory (Merits). Judgment of 12 April 1960. *I.C.J. Reports* (p. 6).

Scovazzi, T. (1996). *Assab, Massaua, Uccialli.* Turin: Giappichelli.

Stuart, G. H. (1931). *The international city of Tangier.* London: Milford.

United Nations. (1950). Treaty of peace with Italy, Paris, 10 February 1947. In *United Nations Treaty Series* (Vol. 49, p. 3).

United Nations. (1951). Anglo-French agreement for the re-establishment of the International Administration of Tangier, Tangier, 31 August 1945. In *United Nations Treaty Series* (Vol. 98, p. 249).

United Nations. (1956). Memorandum of understanding (with annexes and exchange of notes) regarding the Free Territory of Trieste, London, 5 October 1954. In *United Nations Treaty Series* (Vol. 235, p. 99).

United Nations. (1957). Final declaration of the international conference in Tangier and annexed Protocol, Tangier, 29 October 1956. In *United Nations Treaty Series* (Vol. 263, p. 165).

[18]See Chap. 2.

# Part III
# The Industrial Port

# Chapter 6
# The Longshoremen's Organizations

After the XIX century Industrial Revolution, ports grew tremendously in their importance. As noted above,[1] the London Docks became a symbol of the might of the British Empire. In 1889, they were the stage of what was perhaps the first strike in history, the Great Dock Strike.[2]

It is not by chance that the labor movement had one of its defining moments in the Docks. Until some decades ago, goods were shipped as break bulk or packaged cargo. They were loaded from the pier to the ship deck, et vice versa, by dock workers called "longshoremen", and there stowed or unstowed by a different category of dock workers called "stevedores". Dockers, and longshoremen in particular, needed a very specific, in-deep knowledge of the port and its piers: they were highly skilled, difficult to replace workers. Since they were also very cohese, they quickly realized their bargaining power, winning not only excellent collective bargaining agreements, but also local monopolies of dock work for their organizations and a significant participation in the management of the seaport.[3]

This has made ports very locally centered, for various reasons. Longshoremen are very deeply related to their ports in their ethos and job skills. They can better exploit their bargaining power in a strictly local context, rather than being subject to the competition of other ports or dockworkers. The public Authorities and the enterprises confronting the dock organizations, for their part, have no interest in the longshoremen becoming less locally centered and more active participants of international networks of labor relations. This could easily happen—and has indeed partly happened—since longshoremen and seafarers share an established tradition of international unionization, mostly embodied by the International Transport Workers' Federation (ITWF or ITF).[4]

---

[1]Chapter 1.
[2]London Metropolitan Archives (1999).
[3]In many ports, the hegemony of the dockers' organizations lasted until the Nineties, or is still resisting. The significant example of the European ports will be treated under Chap. 13.
[4]Lewis (2003).



M. Casagrande, *Seaports in International Law*, SpringerBriefs in Law,
DOI 10.1007/978-3-319-60396-4_6

However, longshoremen have been much less active on the international playing field, which is accurately mirrored by the neglect of their status by the international labor law.[5]

Today the dock workers' organization consider the internationalization of ports only as a source of social dumping, unfair competition and harassment by shipping multinationals, and they have been strong opponent of any European regulation of the sector.[6] With some exceptions,[7] their labor disputes, initiative, and actions are at the local, regional, or national level.

Since longshoremen still wield significant influence,[8] especially in minor ports, their stance has not helped the development of an international regulation of harbors.

## References

Lewis, H. (2003). *The International Transport Workers' Federation (ITF) 1945–1965: An organizational and political anatomy*. Warwick: University of Warwick.

London Metropolitan Archives. (1999). *The great dock strike, 1889*. Information Leaflet n. 23.

Sanger, D. E., & Greenhouse, S. (2002). President invokes Taft-Hartley Act to open 29 ports. *The New York Times*, 9 October 2002.

South African Transport and Allied Workers' Union. (2008). Satawu Press statement on the Chinese vessel carrying arms/weapons intended for Zimbabwe, released: 17 April 2008.

U.S. House of Representatives. (2017). United States Code. *United States Code*. http://uscode.house.gov/

[5]Chapter 3.

[6]Chapter 13.

[7]In 2008 SATAWU, a ITWF affiliate in South Africa, refused to load or unload the Chinese ship An Yue Jiang, which was allegedly carrying a weapons cargo bound for Zimbabwe. SATAWU stood firm despite the South African Government stating that the ship was allowed to leave since it complied with all the relevant regulations and requirements, and no arms embargo was in force against Zimbabwe anyhow: South African Transport and Allied Workers' Union (2008).

[8]The U.S. longshoremen's organizations were the only trade union against which the federal Government invoked the Labor Management Relations Act of 1947 (better known as Taft-Hartley Act, codified in U.S. House of Representatives (2017), Title 29, Sections 141–197), which empowers the Court to impose a cooling-down period on an ongoing strike. The Act was applied twice, under the Nixon Administration in 1971 but also much more recently, under the Bush jr. Administration in 2002: Sanger and Greenhouse (2002).

# Chapter 7
# The 1923 Geneva Convention on Seaports

Before the entry into force of the Paris Memorandum of Understanding on port State control,[1] the 1923 Geneva Convention on seaports[2] was the only multilateral international treaty specifically regulating ports.

The Convention is the twin treaty of the 1923 Convention on Railways[3]; some articles of the latter are explicitly extended to harbors by the Convention on seaports.[4] The provisions of both Conventions are amalgamated in the 1965 New York Convention.[5]

The Geneva Convention on seaports is a very advanced international instrument whose cornerstone is the equal treatment rule. The port State must grant to ships flying the flag of another Contracting Power the same treatment of its own ships.[6] This obligation is subject to the principle of reciprocity,[7] but this limitation does not apply to such important issues as the levy of customs duties and similar charges.[8]

[1]Chapter 14.

[2]League of Nations (1926–1927). According to the United Nations Treaty Collection database, the Convention is currently in force between Antigua and Barbuda, China, Croatia, Cyprus, Czech Republic, Federal Republic of Germany, Fiji, Ivory Coast, Madagascar, Malaysia, Malta, Marshall Islands, Mauritius, Monaco, Morocco, Nigeria, Slovakia, St. Vincent and the Grenadines, Thailand, Trinidad and Tobago, United Kingdom, Upper Volta, Vanuatu, Yugoslavia and Zimbabwe (ratification table retrieved from https://treaties.un.org/pages/showDetails.aspx?objid=0800000280046b6b). The German Reich was an original signatory of the Convention. West Germany claimed to be the legal successor of the German Reich, and unified Germany in turn claims to be the legal successor of West Germany: von der Dunk and Kooijmans (1991), p. 521ff., 550ff. The Upper Volta is the current Burkina Faso. As for Yugoslavia, it is generally accepted that such State has ceased to exist: United Nations (1992). The treaty is composed of a Convention, a Statute, and a Protocol of Signature, each having a distinct numbering. In this treatise all references are to the articles of the Statute, unless otherwise stated.

[3]League of Nations (1926).

[4]Art. 6 of the Convention on seaports.

[5]United Nations (1967).

[6]Art. 2.

[7]Ibidem.

[8]Art. 5, 19.

 
M. Casagrande, *Seaports in International Law*, SpringerBriefs in Law,
DOI 10.1007/978-3-319-60396-4_7

The equality of treatment can be suspended only as a countermeasure against a Contracting Party not complying with its conventional obligations.[9]

The equal treatment rule, which is a veritable fil rouge within the Convention and is often referenced to in the single provisions, confers to this international instrument a remarkable amount of clarity and internal coherence, without preventing it from addressing some technical, detail issues like port concessions,[10] towage,[11] and pilotage.[12] Such issues are still controversial in the regulation of contemporary ports, which on one hand confirms the advanced characteristics of this Convention, but on the other hand underlines the painfully slow pace of port regulation.

Despite its modernity, anyway, the Convention is not exempt from the systematic shortcomings which are typical of international law when regulating seaports. This emerges clearly in a very important provision of the Convention, laying down the notion of seaport: "All ports which are normally frequented by sea-going vessels and used for foreign trade shall be deemed to be maritime ports within the meaning of the present Statute."[13] The Convention clearly abides to an approach which is typical of the law of seas. The port is considered so strictly as instrumental to the ships[14] that the actual presence of the latter, rather than the abstract suitability to their call, is treated as an intrinsical, constitutive element of the seaport.

The Convention itself implicitly recognizes that this approach is too narrow, and indeed its Protocol recognizes that the treaty applies also to "ports of refuge specially constructed for that purpose."[15] Ports of refuge, which will be treated more extensively further on and which should be more accurately called "places of refuge,"[16] are coastal spots which are used by the coastal State to abide to its international obligation of giving shelter to ships in distress. A place or refuge may, or may not, be a port. The drafters of the Convention realized that, due to the narrow notion of port laid down by the treaty, the latter–and the equal treatment rule it established–would not apply to an installation built specifically to give shelter to ships in distress, and therefore obviously not "normally frequented by sea-going vessels." To deny a right to equal treatment to a ship in distress probably appeared

---

[9]Art. 8 of the Convention. The same article allows the Contracting Party against which such countermeasure is applied to start a summary proceeding before "the Permanent Court of International Justice." The proceeding can now be started before the International Court of Justice pursuant to Article 37 of the Court Statute (International Court of Justice 2017). The summary procedure is still admitted by Article 29 of the Statute (see also Article 15 of the Rules of Court: International Court of Justice 2005).

[10]Art. 2 of the Convention.

[11]Art. 10.

[12]Art. 11.

[13]Art. 1.

[14]See Chap. 3.

[15]Art. 1 of the Protocol of Signature.

[16]See Chap. 11.

so grossly unfair and at odds with maritime customs that the Protocol of Signature was used to avoid such a consequence.

## References

International Court of Justice. (2005). Rules of Court (1978). *International Court of Justice.* http://www.icj-cij.org/documents/index.php?p1=4&p2=3&p3=0

International Court of Justice. (2017). Statute of the International Court of Justice. *International Court of Justice.* http://www.icj-cij.org/documents/?p1=4&p2=2#CHAPTER_II

League of Nations. (1926–1927). Convention and Statute on the International Régime of Maritime Ports, Geneva, 9 December 1923. In *League of Nations Treaty Series* (Vol. 58, p. 285).

League of Nations. (1926). Convention on the international régime of railways, Geneva, 9 December 1923. In *League of Nations Treaty Series* (Vol. 47, p. 55).

United Nations. (1967). Convention on transit trade of land-locked States, New York, 8 July 1965. In *United Nations Treaty Series* (Vol. 597, p. 3).

United Nations. (1992). *Resolution 777 (1992) adopted by the Security Council at its 3116th meeting on 19 September 1992*, S/RES/777.

Von der Dunk, F., & Kooijmans, P. H. (1991). The unification of Germany and International Law. *Michigan Journal of International Law*, 510.

# Chapter 8
# The Forgotten Ports and Port Installations: Lotus Case, Wimbledon Case, Suez Crisis

Ports were involved in some of the most famous international law cases and international crises, but their role was not recognized.

The attitude of overlooking port-related aspects in most relevant international cases is evident in the Wimbledon case. On March 21, 1921 the Wimbledon, a British ship chartered by a French company and loaded with a cargo of weapons bound for Danzig, Poland, asked the German Authorities for permission to cross the Kiel Canal, an artificial waterway linking Brünsbuttel and Kiel, near the border between Germany and Denmark. The permission was denied by Germany pursuant to the international law of neutrality, since Poland was then at war with Russia.

The German position was challenged by the Conference of Ambassadors, since the Treaty of Versailles[1] laid down an obligation of Germany to leave the Canal open to international traffic. Great Britain, France, Italy, and Japan, on one part, and Germany on the other part agreed to submit the case to the newly established Permanent Court of International Justice.[2]

The Court ruled that, despite the fact that neither Poland nor Russia were Parties to the Versailles Treaty, in force of the latter the "Canal has ceased to be an internal and national navigable waterway, the use of which by the vessels of States other than the riparian State is left entirely to the discretion of that State, and that it has become an international waterway intended to provide under treaty guarantee easier access to the Baltic for the benefit of all Nations of the world."[3] Therefore "the passage of neutral vessels carrying contraband of war is authorized by Article 380 [of the Treaty of Versailles], and cannot be imputed to Germany as a failure to fulfil its duties as a neutral. If, therefore, the 'Wimbledon,' making use of the permission

[1]Great Britain (1919).
[2]The facts of the case are summed up by Permanent Court of International Justice (1923), pp. 18–20.
[3]Permanent Court of International Justice (1923), p. 22. The judgement is often cited as evidence of the existence of international treaties establishing objective regimes: Giuliano et alios (1983), p. 412ff., Zamuner (2007), pp. 944, 945.

 
M. Casagrande, *Seaports in International Law*, SpringerBriefs in Law,
DOI 10.1007/978-3-319-60396-4_8

granted it by Article 380, had passed through the Kiel Canal, Germany's neutrality would have remained intact and irreproachable."[4] Germany was thus held in breach of the Versailles Treaty and ordered to compensate France.

Once again, the Court based its entire legal reasoning on the status of the waters of the Canal. However, the Kiel Canal is an artificial waterway regulated by sluices. This means that, in fact, Germany would not have just tolerated the passage of the Wimbledon across its internal waters, but would have had to actively assist it. This fact alone is enough to make at best debatable the statement of the Court that the passage of the Wimbledon would have left German neutrality "intact and irreproachable." Indeed, the core principle of the law of naval neutrality, pursuant to the XIII Hague Convention, is that "the neutrality of a Power is not affected by the mere passage through its territorial waters of war-ships or prizes belonging to belligerents."[5] Any form of assistance by the neutral Power, which is usually justified on humanitarian grounds, is strictly and narrowly regulated by the Convention. The fact that the Court did not even feel expedient to analyze this topic is another example of how the legal regime of the status of waters prevents any consideration on the terrestrial infrastructure serving them.

Another example is the Lotus case decided by the Permanent Court of International Justice. In recent years, this case has returned under the spotlight within the debate on universal jurisdiction.

On August 26, 1926, the French ship S.S. Lotus collided on the high seas with the Turkish ship S.S. Boz-Kourt; precisely, the accident took place off Cape Sigri in the Aegean Sea. The Boz-Kourt sank, while the Lotus reached the harbor of Constantinople; there, the French commander reported the accident to the local French Consul before being arrested on an order issued by the Turkish prosecutor's office in the capital.[6]

France immediately argued that it alone had jurisdiction over a fact involving a ship flying its flag on the high seas, but the argument was rejected by a Turkish Court. In 1926 France and Turkey agreed to submit the case to the Permanent Court of International Justice. In 1927, the Court ruled that Turkey had jurisdiction over the maritime accident since "what occurs on board a vessel on the high seas must be regarded as if it occurred on the territory of the State whose flag the ship flies. If, therefore, a guilty act committed on the high seas produces its effects on a vessel flying another flag or in foreign territory, the same principles must be applied as if the territories of two different States were concerned, and the conclusion must therefore be drawn that there is no rule of international law prohibiting the State to which the ship on which the effects of the offence have taken place belongs, from

---

[4]Permanent Court of International Justice (1923), pp. 29, 30.

[5]International Committee of the Red Cross (2017), Article 10. The law of maritime neutrality will be further treated under Chap. 9.

[6]The facts of the case are summed up by Permanent Court of International Justice (1927), pp. 10, 11.

regarding the offence as having been committed in its territory and prosecuting, accordingly, the delinquent."[7]

It can be noticed that the call of the French ship in the Turkish port of Constantinople was never taken into consideration or considered relevant in the legal reasoning of the parts and of the Court, not even as a basis to establish at least a precautionary jurisdiction of Turkey; a jurisdiction limited, for example, to the inspection of the ship, the interrogation of the commander, of the crew and of the Turkish survivors rescued by the French ship. No legal relevance was attached to the presence of the French ship within the Turkish port.

It is also relevant that the judgement was met with a storm of diplomatic criticism for allegedly violating the prerogatives of the flag State,[8] finally leading to the adoption of the 1958 Geneva Convention,[9] according to which "in the event of a collision or of any other incident of navigation concerning a ship on the high seas, involving the penal or disciplinary responsibility of the master or of any other person in the service of the ship, no penal or disciplinary proceedings may be instituted against such persons except before the judicial or administrative authorities either of the flag State or of the State of which such person is a national."[10] The adoption of such a strong position by the international community is still affecting the contemporary law of the sea and practice regarding the status of foreign ships in seaports.[11]

Finally, the third case involves another internationalized canal, id est the Suez Canal. Pursuant to the 1888 Constantinople Convention,[12] "the Suez Maritime Canal shall always be free and open, in time of was as in time of peace, to every vessel of commerce or of war, without distinction of flag. Consequently, the High Contracting Parties agree not in any ways to interfere with the free use of the Canal, in time of was as in time of peace. The Canal shall never be subjected to the exercise of the right of blockade."[13] In 1957, Egypt filled with the United Nations Secretariat a declaration committing itself to maintain the internationalized status of the Canal.[14] However, since 1949 Egypt had enforced a blockade against Israel,[15] and after the 1967 Six Days War the Canal was closed completely until 1975.[16]

The Canal was the epicenter of a well-known international crisis in 1956, when Egypt unilaterally nationalized the Canal—or rather, once again, the installations

---

[7]Permanent Court of International Justice (1927), p. 25.

[8]Ozcayir (2004), pp. 86, 87.

[9]United Nations (1963).

[10]Article 11, paragraph 1 of the Convention.

[11]Chapter 14.

[12]Suez Canal Authority (2008). Until 1914, Egypt was de jure a province of the Ottoman Empire, despite having been de facto independent at least since 1805.

[13]Article I of the Convention.

[14]United Nations (1957).

[15]United Nations (1951).

[16]Lapidoth (1976).

serving it—from the Compagnie universelle du canal maritime de Suez, a French corporation which was de facto under British control.[17] Beside controlling the corporation, Great Britain was also granted extensive rights over the Canal—or rather the installations serving it and the network of military bases guarding it—by the 1954 Anglo-Egyptian Agreement.[18] After the Agreement, Britain had evacuated its military bases in the Canal area, but had reserved the right to reoccupy them "in the event of an armed attack."[19] The British Royal Air Force had the right to use the bases and installations,[20] which were guarded by civilian guards employed by British contractors.[21]

The Egyptian expropriation led Britain to launch a full-scale retaliatory military operation against Egypt, supported by France and Israel. The operation obviously appeared unlawful in light of the Charter of the United Nations, and the issue was debated, within the British Government, by the Lord Chancellor and the Law Officers.[22] The latter challenged the view of the Lord Chancellor, according to whom a British military intervention against Egypt would have been in compliance with the UN Charter since it would have been aimed at protecting vital national interests and British citizens abroad.[23] Still, the interpretation of international law given by the Law Officers was not very strict, so much that, in their opinion, an armed intervention would have been justified if Egypt had closed the Canal to ships flying the British flag.[24] In doing so, Egypt would have forcefully attempted to take control of an internationalized waterway whose status could be lawfully defended even by using the military force. Even in this case, therefore, the Law Officers focused all their attention on the waters of the Canal, without taking in any consideration the status of the facilities serving it; and yet, since the United Kingdom was the holder of sovereign rights over those facilities, their forced appropriation by Egypt could have been another argument—no weaker than the one put forward by the Law Officers—to justify a military reaction as self-defense. There are at least some elements in the international practice, jurisprudence and doctrine suggesting

[17]The British Government owned 44 percent of the shares of the company. Deney (1967), p. 294. The corporation survived the crisis and its legal successor Engie (formerly known as GDF Suez) is currently at the head of a corporate group of the same name: Agence France-Presse (2015).

[18]United Nations (1955).

[19]Article 4 of the Agreement.

[20]Article 7 of the Agreement.

[21]Annex II, Part E, Article 3(a) of the Agreement.

[22]The Lord Chancellor and Secretary of State for Justice is the British Minister of Justice; before the British constitutional reform of 2005 (by the Constitutional Reform Act 2005), the Lord Chancellor also performed judicial functions. The Law Officers are the Attorney General and the Solicitor General. They tender legal advice to the British Government and oversee its prosecution services.

[23]Marston (1988), pp. 782, 783. The British citizens referred to by the Lord Chancellor were the British employees of the Compagnie Universelle. The Egyptian law nationalizing the Canal compelled all the Company employees to carry on their duty, which was considered as some sort of forced labor by the Lord Chancellor.

[24]Marston (1988), p. 786.

that the right of self-defense can be invoked not only in case of an armed attack against the territory of a State, but also if such attack targets State assets abroad: such assets could be ships, as speculated by the Law Officers, but also aircrafts, military bases, embassies, oil platforms, etc.[25]

## References

Agence France-Presse. (2015). *De la Compagnie universelle du canal de Suez à Engie*, 24 April 2015.

Ago, R. (1980). *Addendum to the eighth report on State responsibility*. A/CN.4/318/ADD.5-7.

Deney, N. (1967). L'Égypte et la compagnie universelle du canal maritime de Suez. *Revue française de science politique, 17*, 293.

Giuliano, M., et al. (1983). *Diritto internazionale* (II ed., Vol. I, p. 265, 266). Milan: Giuffrè.

Great Britain. (1919). *The Treaty of Peace between the Allied and Associated Powers and Germany, the Protocol annexed thereto, the Agreement respecting the military occupation of the territories of the Rhine, and the Treaty between France and Great Britain respecting assistance to France in the event of unprovoked aggression by Germany. Signed at Versailles, June 28th, 1919*. London: H.M. Stationery Office.

International Committee of the Red Cross. (2017). Convention (XIII) concerning the rights and duties of neutral Powers in naval war. The Hague, 18 October 1907. *ICRC*. https://www.icrc.org/applic/ihl/ihl.nsf/INTRO/240

International Court of Justice. (2003). Case concerning oil platforms. Judgment of 6 November 2003. *I.C.J. Reports* (p. 161).

Lapidoth, R. (1976). The reopened Suez Canal in International Law. *Syracuse Journal of International Law and Commerce, 4*, 149.

Marston, G. (1988). Armed intervention in the 1957 Suez Canal Crisis. *International & Comparative Law Quarterly*, 773.

Ozcayir, O. (2004). *Port State Control* (II ed.). London-Singapore: Informa Professionals.

Permanent Court of International Justice. (1923). Case of the S.S. "Wimbledon", Series A01, p. 11.

Permanent Court of International Justice. (1927). The case of the S.S. "Lotus", Series A10, p. 4.

Suez Canal Authority. (2008). Costantinople Convention. *Suez Canal*. http://www.suezcanal.gov.eg/sc.aspx?show=37

United Nations. (1951). *Resolution 95 (1951) adopted by the Security Council at its 549th meeting on 26 July 1951*, S/2322.

United Nations. (1955). Agreement between the Government of the Republic of Egypt and the Government of the United Kingdom of Great Britain and Northern Ireland, Cairo, 19 October 1954. In *United Nations Treaty Series* (Vol. 210, p. 22).

United Nations. (1957). Declaration on the Suez Canal and the arrangements for its operations, Cairo, 24 April 1957. In *United Nations Treaty Series* (Vol. 269, p. 299).

United Nations. (1963). Convention on the high seas, Geneva, 29 April 1958. In *United Nations Treaty Series* (Vol. 450, p. 11).

Zamuner, E. (2007). I trattati che creano regimi obiettivi nel diritto internazionale. *Comunicazioni e Studi, XXIII*, 941.

[25]International Court of Justice (2003), and Ago (1980), pp. 67, 68.

# Chapter 9
# When You are Forced to Remember the Port: The Laws of Wars from the Hague Conventions to the Cuban Crisis

The international law of naval warfare is generally attentive enough to seaports, which it treats adopting a quite pragmatic approach, imposed by the harsh necessities of warfare.

Seaports are mentioned in the III, VI, VIII, IX, and XIII Hague Conventions[1] and in the II Geneva Convention,[2] which lay down the rules of naval warfare regarding ports in general and neutral ports in particular. A common, and highly significant trait of all the said international instruments is their lack of distinction between civilian and military ports. This is not surprising, since ports of both kinds can be used by warships to refit, refuel, etc.

Indeed, what is probably the most famous case in which the XIII Hague Convention was applied, the Graf von Spee case, took place in the civilian harbor of Montevideo, Uruguay. Such port was used as a place of refuge by the German warship Graf von Spee, which had been seriously damaged by British ships, in December 1939. Uruguay was then a neutral Power.[3] Pursuant to the XIII Hague Convention, "a belligerent warship may not prolong its stay in a neutral port beyond the permissible time except on account of damage or stress of weather. It must depart as soon as the cause of the delay is at an end."[4] A Uruguayan Government Commission therefore inspected the German ship and fixed in three days the time which was considered strictly necessary for the repair of the ship. At the expiration of this short term, the ship was ordered to leave the Uruguayan waters. Soon after abandoning the harbor the ship, which was now able to sail but not to face the British flotilla waiting for her off Montevideo, was scuttled by the crew.[5]

---

[1]International Committee of the Red Cross (2017b, c, d, e, f).
[2]International Committee of the Red Cross (2017a).
[3]Uruguay declared war against Germany and Japan only in 1945: República Oriental del Uruguay (1945).
[4]International Committee of the Red Cross (2017f), Article 14.
[5]McDougal and Feliciano (1994), p. 461. The Uruguayan Government almost immediately published a Blue Book on the case: Uruguayan Government (1940).



M. Casagrande, *Seaports in International Law*, SpringerBriefs in Law,
DOI 10.1007/978-3-319-60396-4_9

The most important institution of the law of naval warfare, however, is undoubtedly the blockade. In a blockade, a belligerent Power deploys its navy to completely stop the maritime traffic from and to an enemy port.[6] A blockade must be both formally declared and effective; it applies to belligerent as well as neutral ships. It has traditionally been considered an actual use of armed force against the blockaded State, rather than a threat of using armed force.[7]

Historically, the blockade was put into effect by the blockading Power by physically occupying the port waters with its warships (proximity blockade). After the development of coast defenses, in particular coast artillery, made such a deployment impossible, the blockade became the task of flotillas watching the sea lanes to and from the port in the high seas.

If the warships guarding the sea lanes from and to the port are not instructed to stop any ship suspected of calling to the port, but rather to inspect such ships and inspect their cargo for forbidden goods (usually weapons, ammunition or military supplies), what they are enforcing is not a blockade but rather a quarantine.

A quarantine is simply a form of exercise of the belligerent right of visit and search in order to prevent contraband, id est the delivery of certain goods (usually of a military nature or utility, as said above) to the enemy. In a quarantine, such right is exercised by guarding the routes to a given enemy port rather than via a generic activity of sea patrol.

The concepts of blockade and quarantine became of paramount importance during the 1962 Cuban crisis. The Soviet Union had built on the Caribbean island, with the consent of the Cuban Government, some launching sites for nuclear warheads missiles. The Cuban-Soviet operation had obviously been kept secret, but had been detected by the U.S. intelligence. The United States reacted by imposing a quarantine on the delivery of military supplies to Cuba.[8] This way, the United

[6]During the American Civil War, the U.S. Government argued that a blockade can, under given conditions, be applied also to neutral ports, but this doctrine has remained isolated: Department of the Navy (2007), Section 7.7.4; Ministry of Defence (2014), paragraph 13.65ff; International Law Association (1998), paragraph 5.2.10; International Committee of the Red Cross (2017h), Article 99. More recently, Israel declared a blockade in the framework of its alleged "war" against Hamas: The public Commission to examine the maritime incident of 31 May 2010 (2011); United Nations General Assembly (2010).

[7]Qualifying the blockade as an actual use of armed force can obviously give way to the exercise of the right of self-defense by the blockaded State. Such a legal consequence can appear extreme, at least insofar no distinction is drawn between the total blockade of an insular State which has no other means of supplying its population and the blockade of some ports of a State which can be supplied by land. Indeed there are at least some doubts on the possibility to consider a blockade as an armed attack pursuant to the UN Charter, but this has not been ruled out altogether: Ruys (2010), p. 275ff.

[8]In his televised speech of 22 October 1962, U.S. President John F. Kennedy clearly outlined the difference between quarantine and blockade: text of the speech retrieved from Van Doren and McHenry (1971), p. 582. See also Allison (1999), p. 111ff.

States avoided to adopt a behavior which, legally, was still widely considered an actual use of force against Cuba.[9]

With a very harsh letter signed by First Secretary[10] Nikita S. Khrushchev in person, the Soviet Union simply noticed that the quarantine violated the international law of the sea and constituted a threat of use of force against the Soviet Union, as embodied in the ships flying its flag.[11] The Soviet reaction embarrassed the United States, which counterposed weak legal arguments, such as a multilateral revamping of the Monroe Doctrine under the aegis of the Organization of American States.[12]

This episode of the Cuban crisis, which ended in Russia's retirement of its missiles, is significant as it reveals as, when international law has to regulate the pressing necessities of war, its consideration of the relationship between the port and the sea becomes more balanced. Apparently, the legal regulation of the blockade is no exception to the ordinary approach maintained by the law of the sea. The port is still an accessory to the waters, so much that a conduct by a State in the high seas is considered as an act against the port State. And yet, for the first time the port becomes the most important component of the port–sea relationship, so much that the State conduct in the high seas is evaluated primarily as a violation of the rights of the port State, overlooking the—usually obsessively safeguarded—rights of the flag States.

Once again, this change in perspective is forced into international law by the concrete interests to be regulated. In the case of a naval blockade, it is painfully clear that the real target of this particular instrument of warfare are not the (neutral) States whose ship are sailing in the seas under blockade, but rather the port State[13] which could be—literally—starved into submission.[14]

---

[9]As far as the United States knew, Cuba could have been delivered the launch codes of the nuclear missiles by the Soviet authorities. This was not the case, as it was proven in 2002 by Russian Federation (2002). The U.S. Joint Chiefs of Staff assessed that the risk of a nuclear attack from Cuba was so high that they recommended an immediate invasion of the island: Kennedy (1971), p. 14. Also the French President Charles de Gaulle advised the United States that the quarantine was not an adequate counter-move: Department of State (1962).

[10]First Secretary of the Central Committee of the Communist Party of the Soviet Union and Chairman of the Council of Ministers of the Union of the Soviet Socialist Republics.

[11]John F. Kennedy Presidential Library and Museum (2017).

[12]Abel (1966), p. 44; Oliver and Tondel (1964), p. 26.

[13]The blockade is sometimes described as targeting the coast, rather than the ports, of a State. However, no meaningful supplying is possible but via the seaports, which must therefore be considered the real target of any blockade.

[14]The reciprocal blockade between Great Britain and Germany during World War I was officially qualified by both Powers as maritime patrolling against war contraband: Department of State (2017); Ambassador Gerard to the Secretary of State (Telegram), 4 May 1916, retrieved from Lutz (1932). However, they were de facto blockades, so much that specific "war zones" for the interception of enemy and neutral ships were designated in the Northern and Baltic Sea and around the British Isles, respectively. As for the kind of cargo transported by the ships, the British Government adopted lists of forbidden goods which were so ample as to include virtually any good, including food, while the German submarines were obviously unable to inspect the ships.

## References

Abel, E. (1966). *La crisi dei missili.* Milan: Garzanti. Translation of Abel, E. (1966). *The missile crisis.* New York: Bantam.

Allison, G. T. (1999). *Essence of decision* (2nd ed.). New York: Longman.

Department of State. (1962). *Telegram from the Embassy in France to the Department of State*, Central Files, 611.3722/10-2262.

Department of the Navy. (2007). *The Commander's handbook on the law of naval operations*, Edition July 2007, NWP 1–14M.

Department of State. (2017). *The secretary of state to the ambassador in Great Britain*, File No. 763.72112/545a.

International Committee of the Red Cross. (2017a). Convention (II) for the amelioration of the condition of wounded, sick and shipwrecked members of armed forces at sea, Geneva, 12 August 1949. *ICRC.* https://www.icrc.org/ihl/INTRO/370?OpenDocument

International Committee of the Red Cross. (2017b). Convention (III) relative to the opening of hostilities, The Hague, 18 October 1907. *ICRC.* Retrieved from: https://www.icrc.org/ihl/INTRO/190?OpenDocument

International Committee of the Red Cross. (2017c). Convention (VI) relating to the status of enemy merchant ships at the outbreak of hostilities, The Hague, 18 October 1907. *ICRC.* https://www.icrc.org/applic/ihl/ihl.nsf/Treaty.xsp?documentId=250D6DDD0DACDCD7C12563CD002D67CD&action=openDocument

International Committee of the Red Cross. (2017d). Convention (VIII) relative to the laying of automatic submarine contact mines, The Hague, 18 October 1907. *ICRC.* https://www.icrc.org/applic/ihl/ihl.nsf/INTRO/215

International Committee of the Red Cross. (2017e). Convention (IX) concerning bombardment by naval forces in time of war, The Hague, 18 October 1907. *ICRC.* https://www.icrc.org/applic/ihl/ihl.nsf/Treaty.xsp?action=openDocument&documentId=F13F9FFC628FC33BC12563CD002D6819

International Committee of the Red Cross. (2017f). Convention (XIII) concerning the rights and duties of neutral Powers in naval war. The Hague, 18 October 1907, *ICRC.* https://www.icrc.org/applic/ihl/ihl.nsf/INTRO/240

International Committee of the Red Cross. (2017g). Procès-verbal relating to the rules of submarine warfare set forth in Part IV of the Treaty of London of 22 April 1930, London, 6 November 1936. *ICRC.* https://www.icrc.org/applic/ihl/ihl.nsf/Article.xsp?action=openDocument&documentId=C103186F0C4291EEC12563CD00519832

International Committee of the Red Cross. (2017h). San Remo Manual on International Law Applicable to Armed Conflicts at Sea. *ICRC.* https://www.icrc.org/ihl/INTRO/560?OpenDocument

International Law Association. (1998). *Report of the Sixty-Eight Conference, International Law Association*, London, 1998, p. 496: "Helsinki Principles on the law of maritime neutrality".

(Footnote 14 continued)

The same can be said of the unrestricted submarine warfare waged by Germany against Britain during World War II. Again, the judgment passed by the International Military Tribunal against Grand Admiral Karl Dönitz, Commander-in-Chief of the German Navy from 1943 to 1945, makes references to the Second London Protocol (International Committee of the Red Cross 2017g) regulating contraband (Rule 2 of the Protocol): International Military Tribunal (Nuremberg) (1946). However, the very same judgment records that the submarine warfare campaign was waged, or at least focused, within "operational zones." Once again, the use of submarines meant that the ships were not inspected, therefore no distinction was made between contraband and noncontraband cargoes.

International Military Tribunal (Nuremberg). (1946). *Trial of the Major War Criminals before the International Military Tribunal.* International Military Tribunal (Nuremberg): Nuremberg, 14 November 1945–1 October 1946, Volume XXII, p. 3: "Judgment of 1 October 1946".

John F. Kennedy Presidential Library and Museum. (2017). Letter from Chairman Khrushchev to President Kennedy, 24 October 1962. *John F. Kennedy Presidential Library and Museum.* http://microsites.jfklibrary.org/cmc/oct24/doc2.html

Kennedy, R. (1971). *Thirteen Days.* New York: W.W. Norton.

Lutz, R. H. (1932). *Fall of the German Empire* (1st ed.). Stanford-London: Stanford University Press-Oxford University Press.

McDougal, M. S., & Feliciano, F. P. (1994). *The International Law of War.* New Haven-Dordrecht-Boston-London: New Haven Press-Martinus Nijhoff Publishers.

Ministry of Defence. (2014). *The joint service manual of the law of armed conflict*, JSP 383.

Oliver, C. L., & Tondel, L. (1964). *The Inter-American Security System and the Cuban Crisis.* New York: Dobbs Ferry.

República Oriental del Uruguay. (1945). *Ley No. 10.602.* Montevideo: República Oriental del Uruguay.

Russian Federation. (2002). *Telegram TROSTNIK (REED-USSR Defense Minister Rodion Malinovsky), to PAVLOV (Commander of the Group of Soviet Forces in Cuba general Isa Pliev), 27 October 1962.* Archive of the President of the Russian Federation, Special Declassification, April 2002.

Ruys, T. (2010). *'Armed attack' and Article 51 of the UN Charter.* Cambridge: Cambridge University Press.

The Public Commission to Examine the Maritime Incident of the 31st of May 2010. (2011). *Report.* Government Printing: Jerusalem.

United Nations General Assembly. (2010). *Report of the international fact-finding mission to investigate violations of international law, including international humanitarian law and human rights law, resulting from the Israeli attacks on the flotilla of ships carrying humanitarian assistance*, A/HRC/15/21.

Van Doren, C. L., & McHenry, R. (Eds.). (1971). *Webster's guide to American history.* Springfield: Merriam-Webster.

# Chapter 10
# The Mar del Plata Convention

In addition to the Geneva Convention on seaports,[1] another multilateral treaty exists which, despite being regional and dedicated more broadly to maritime transport, lays down significant provision relating to harbors. This instrument is the 1963 Mar del Plata Convention,[2] which was stipulated in the framework of the Organization of American States.

Particularly noteworthy is Article 4 of the Convention, granting the Inter-American Port and Harbor Conference the power to "adopt and amend inter-American standards and recommended practices dealing with all matters relating to formalities, requirements and procedures relevant to the efficient and economic entry and clearance of vessels, and the expeditious and appropriate treatment of their passengers, crew, cargo and baggage." It is unclear whether the standards and recommended practices adopted by the Conference are legally binding or just soft law rules. The Convention seems to treat them as hard law rules insofar as it provides for them to become "an Annex" to the Convention itself.[3] However, apparently the only consequence for a State unwilling to abide to a standard or recommended practice is an obligation to motivate such decision to the General Secretariat,[4] which rather suggests that we are dealing with soft law rules. Another possibility would be classifying the standards and recommended practice as technical rules such as those adopted by international organizations having a technical mission like IMO, WHO or ICAO. The exact nature of these technical rules is debated.[5] However, technical rules are usually complied with by their by their intended subjects, independently from their legal nature, due to standardization

[1]See above, Chap. 7.
[2]Organization of American States (2017).
[3]Article 5(c). The standards and recommended practices become part of the Convention at the date or their entry into force, which cannot be set by the Convention before three months from their adoption, "unless, in the meantime, a majority of the Contracting States notify their disapproval to the General Secretariat of the Organization of American States: Article 5(b).
[4]Article 6.
[5]Giuliano et al. (1983), pp. 265, 266, Quadri (1968), p. 72.



M. Casagrande, *Seaports in International Law*, SpringerBriefs in Law,
DOI 10.1007/978-3-319-60396-4_10

and mutual recognition exigencies, whilst the wording of the Mar del Plata Convention clearly assumes that the compliance to the standards and recommended practices by a Contracting State will be based solely on its goodwill and its evaluation of the impact of an inter-American rule on its port system.[6]

The issue of the exact nature of the rules adopted under the Mar del Plata Convention is merely academic anyway, since the rule-making procedure established by the treaty has never been implemented. In 1988, the Port and Harbor Conference was simply dissolved for not having "an organizational plan to govern its structure and functioning that has been approved by the General Assembly" and replaced by a Special Inter-American Committee on Ports.[7] Pursuant to its Rules of Procedure,[8] the Committee cannot adopt rules or recommended practices; whenever common rules are deemed necessary, the Committee promotes the negotiation of an ad hoc international agreement.[9]

On a background of ports neglected by international law and kept under domestic jurisdiction by States and port clusters, the stipulation of the Mar del Plata Convention is the exception, and its lack of implementation the rule. Indeed, this international instrument was born in a very peculiar political context created by the Cold War. The Mar del Plata Convention is the first multilateral agreement concluded in the framework of OAS after the famous San José Declaration,[10] adopted by the Organization in 1960, in reaction to the Cuban Revolution, as a clear anti-communist statement.[11] The Declaration was adopted at the San José Meeting of Consultation of Ministers of Foreign Affairs, which approved a broader agenda of continental integration—including economic integration—,[12] which de facto reaffirmed the U.S. hegemony over the Western hemisphere, and therefore was regarded as a hostile act by Cuba and as an unfriendly act by the Communist countries, but—it can be speculated—as too invasive even by some Latin American countries.[13] In order to prove that the San José Declaration had produced some concrete commitment by the OAS Member States, ports were probably chosen as a topic with the tacit understanding that their usual lack of an international regulation,

---

[6]"Any State which finds it impracticable to comply with the inter-American standard or to bring its own regulations or practices into full accord with any such standard…:" Art. 6(a).

[7]Organization of American States (1998).

[8]Organization of American States (2013).

[9]The list of the cooperation agreements stipulated under the aegis of the Committee can be retrieved from: http://www.oas.org/cip/english/cooperagree.html. Such agreements, moreover, generally establish procedures of inter-institutional cooperation between OAS and other national or international entities, rather than laying down common rules. The aforesaid list, moreover, reveals that the dissolved Port and Harbor Conference had promoted only one international agreement: Organization of American States (1974).

[10]Organization of American States (1960).

[11]Cuba issued a counter-declaration, the so-called "First Havana Declaration:" Partido Comunista de Cuba (2011).

[12]Organization of American States (1960).

[13]Saull (2001), p. 185.

on one hand, made them a less relevant and sensitive issue; on the other hand, the very same lack of international precedents and practice would have sterilized the implementation of the Convention, as in fact it was the case.[14]

## References

Angosto-Ferrández, L. F. (Ed.). (2014). *Democracy, revolution and geopolitics in Latin America*. New York-London: Routledge.

Giuliano, M., et al. (1983). *Diritto internazionale* (2nd ed., Vol. 1). Milan: Giuffrè.

Henderson, J. D., et al. (2000). *A reference guide to Latin American history*. Armonk-New York-London: M.E. Shape.

Organization of American States. (1960). *Seventh meeting of consultation of ministers of foreign affairs—Final act*. Washington, DC: Pan American Union.

Organization of American States. (1962). *Eighth meeting of consultation of ministers of foreign affairs—Final act*. Washington, DC: Pan American Union.

Organization of American States. (1974). *Agreement for co-operation between the inter-governmental Maritime Consultative Organization and the Organization of American States, London, 2 October 1974*, OEA/Ser.B/VIII.19-74.

Organization of American States. (1998). *Proposal to transform the Inter-American Port and Harbor Conference into the Inter-American Ports Commission*, AG/RES. 1573 (XXVIII-O/98).

Organization of American States. (2013). *Rules of Procedure of the Inter-American Committee on Ports (CIP)*. OEA/Ser.W CIDI/doc.59/13, 3 June 2013, official translation from Spanish.

Organization of American States. (2017). Inter-American Convention on facilitation of international waterborne transportation (Convention of Mar del Plata). *OAS*. http://www.oas.org/juridico/english/treaties/b-30.html

Partido Comunista de Cuba. (2011). "Primera Declaración de La Habana", *PCC*. http://www.pcc.cu/pdf/documentos/otros_doc/primera_declaracion_habana.pdf

Quadri, R. (1968). *Diritto internazionale pubblico* (5th ed., p. 72). Naples: Liguori.

Saull, R. (2001). *Rethinking theory and history in the cold war*. London-Portland: Frank Cass.

[14]The entire economic agenda adopted at the San José Meeting, which become collectively known as the "Alliance for Progress", was ultimately abandoned in the Seventies: Henderson et al. (2000), p. 225. The U.S. aim of containing or isolating Cuba was instead fully achieved at the 1962 Punta del Este Meeting, which led to the suspension of Cuba from OAS: Organization of American States (1962). See Angosto-Ferrández (2014), p. 22.

# Chapter 11
# The Montego Bay Convention

Dating back to 1982, the United Nations Convention on the Law of the Sea, also known as the Montego Bay Convention, is still the most important international instrument codifying and integrating the law of the sea.

In the whole Convention only three, albeit significant, provisions are dedicated to seaports: Article 11 on the relevance of seaports in the delimitation of territorial sea, Article 131 on the equal treatment of ships within ports, and Article 218 on port State jurisdiction ("port State enforcement" in the wording of the Convention).

Article 131 and 218 will be treated first, since Article 11 requires a more in deep analysis.

Is should be noted that Article 131 does not regulate the treatment of all ships by a port State, but rather forbids any discrimination against ships flying the flag of a land-locked State, thus adopting a rather narrow approach. In fact, Article 131 should be read together to Article 125 of the Convention, regulating to right to access to the sea of land-locked States.[1] Paragraph 1 of Article 125 reads: "Land-locked States shall have the right of access to and from the sea for the purpose of exercising the rights provided for in this Convention including those relating to the freedom of the high seas and the common heritage of mankind. To this end, land-locked States shall enjoy freedom of transit through the territory of transit States by all means of transport". It appears therefore that Article 131 was inserted in the Convention mainly to clarify that ships flying the flag of land-locked States—just like any other foreign ship[2]—do not have a right to access to a seaport.

Article 218 regulates the exercise of jurisdiction by the port State over a foreign ship, limiting such exercise on subjective and objective grounds.

Subjectively, the ship must have entered the port "voluntarily".[3] This requirement echoes the traditional argument according to which is jurisdiction of the port State over a foreign ship is based on the consent of the flag State, as manifested by

[1]Nordquist et al. (1995), pp. 373–374.
[2]See Chap. 16.
[3]Paragraph 1.



M. Casagrande, *Seaports in International Law*, SpringerBriefs in Law,
DOI 10.1007/978-3-319-60396-4_11

the captain of the ship acting in his capacity as a organ of the flag State.[4] Therefore, if the entry in the port was involuntary, such as in the case of a ship in distress, such ship is exempt from the jurisdiction of the port State.[5]

Objectively, the jurisdiction of the port State appears limited by the Convention to some very specific violations of international environmental law, and precisely "any discharge from that vessel outside the internal waters, territorial sea or exclusive economic zone of that State in violation of applicable international rules and standards established through the competent international organization or general diplomatic conference".[6] This provision aims at offering some narrow exception to the very strict standards established in the international practice after the Lotus case.[7]

A contrario, however, the norm confirms that, outside the very specific case of a "discharge", the port State is not entitled to exercise its jurisdiction over a foreign ship for any fact which took place outside its territorial waters or Exclusive Economic Zone[8]; and, at the same time, that the port State can exercise its jurisdiction in relation to facts which took place, or have taken place, within its territorial waters, such as the violation of international maritime standards. Within this not so broad area of port State jurisdiction, it is possible to demarcate an even more restricted, but very relevant area: port State control (PSC). Since PSC is regulated by norms which are not found in the Montego Bay or even in the law of the sea, it will be treated separately further on.[9] For now, it will suffice to highlight that the Montego Bay Convention, despite having been subject to significant integrations after its adoption in 1982, was never amended or expanded in order to cover PSC.

It is now finally possible to examine Article 11, a little known provision which regulates ports with respect to the delimitation of territorial waters. Article 11 is considered particularly important in this treatise, since the legal notion of where the port ends and the open sea begins, and of the relation existing between port and

[4]Lauterpacht (editor) (1948), p. 43.

[5]Yang (2006), p. 66; Bardin (2002), p. 31; *contra* Molenaar (1998), pp. 101ff. Beside distress, the foreign ship could be forced or tricked by the State into entering its port. According to some sources, the latter applies to the Italian tanker Enrica Lexie, who originated the well-know international dispute between Italy and India (Mannucci 2014, pp. 117–118). For that dispute, a judicial proceeding is currently pending in the International Tribunal for the Law of the Sea. In its written pleadings, Italy argued that the ship was "forced to enter Indian territorial waters" (International Tribunal for the Law of the Sea 2015a, paragraph 21). In its Order of 24 August 2015 (International Tribunal for the Law of the Sea 2015b), the Tribunal did not offer significant elements on the merits of the controversy, being content with stating that "both Parties have sufficiently demonstrated that the rights they seek to protect regarding the Enrica Lexie incident are plausible" (*ibid*, paragraph 85).

[6]Art. 218, paragraph 1.

[7]*Supra*, Chap. 8.

[8]The "grey zone" of the coastal State jurisdiction over its Exclusive Economic Area would require a specific examination, which cannot be undertaken herein.

[9]See Chap. 14.

open water, can be considered the litmus test of what the port is in the international legal order.

Article 11 reads: "For the purpose of delimiting the territorial sea, the outermost permanent harbour works which form an integral part of the harbour system are regarded as forming part of the coast. Off-shore installations and artificial islands shall not be considered as permanent harbour works". The provision is apparently clear, but in practice it has proven difficult to establish what is "an integral part of the harbor system" and to distinguish such installations from "off-shore installations".[10] The issue is likely to be risen again in the future, since more and more ports, in order to handle the ever-growing size of container ships, are planning to build extensions into the sea. The port of Venice, for example, is planning to create not mere offshore installations, but a second offshore port.[11]

However, in this case the uncertain legal regime applying to ports is not the consequence of a lack of focus on the issue by the law of the sea. Rather, it should be acknowledged that the law of sea in general has yet to grasp how to regulate the artificial alteration of the coast with respect to waters delimitation. Probably, it has been problematic to reach an international consensus on this issue, since, on one hand, some degree of artificial alteration of the coast is unavoidable; on the other hand, States fear that such alterations—allowed by contemporary technology on an increasingly massive scale—could be exploited by coastal States to push forward their baseline. The growing practice of land reclamation is emblematic of the potential interests at stake,[12] but legal problems have been raised also by less impacting projects such as bridges.[13]

---

[10]In order to establish whether or not a given port work could be used as a baseline, different criteria were applied: the position of the work with respect to the low-water line (Shalowitz and Reed 2000, pp. 190ff.), the work purpose (International Court of Justice 2009, paragraph 132; Fietta and Cleverly 2015, p. 483; Tanaka 2012, p. 62), equity and reasonableness (Churchill and Lowe 1988, p. 40; Kolb 2003, pp. 144–145).

[11]Venice Port Authority (2010).

[12]A forerunner in the practice of land reclamation was the Principality of Monaco, which in the Sixties of the XX century artificially created Fontvieille, an entirely new district of Montecarlo. In 1984 a convention between Monaco and France (United Nations 1985) tacitly neutralized any possible impact of Fontvieille on the delimitation of the territorial waters of the Principality, by delimitating such waters according to specific geographic coordinates and more generally stating that "les eaux territoriales monégasques ont la même largeur que les eaux territoriales françaises" (Art. 1, n. 3). The practice related to the Fontvieille case, however, is too isolated to be conclusive, also because it is influenced by the special relationship existing between Monaco and France. In general, the legal effects of land reclamation for the purpose of waters delimitation are not yet fully clear (Symmons 2005, p. 65). Some clarification could be offered by a specific case between Malaysia and Singapore, pending in the International Tribunal of the Law of the Sea (International Tribunal for the Law of the Sea 2003).

[13]According to the Judge Advocate General of the U.S. Coast Guard and the legal department of the U.S. Immigration and Naturalization Service, the Seven Miles Bridge connecting Florida with the Florida Keys Island must be considered as U.S. territory, except for some abandoned, disconnected segments. The position taken by the Coast Guard and INS is quoted in U.S. District Court, S.D. Florida. Miami Division (2006). Conversely, the 1991 treaty between Sweden and

In this context, it is worth mentioning the international practice triggered by the U.S. Deepwater Port Act,[14] a 1974 federal Act regulating the construction and operation of deepwater ports, meaning "any fixed or floating manmade structure other than a vessel, or any group of such structures, that are located beyond State seaward boundaries and that are used or intended for use as a port or terminal for the transportation, storage, or further handling of oil or natural gas for transportation to or from any State".[15]

The provisions of the Act are introduced by a "Congressional declaration of policy" in which "the Congress declares that nothing in this chapter shall be construed to affect the legal status of the high seas, the superjacent airspace, or the seabed and subsoil, including the Continental Shelf". The Act, moreover, acknowledge that "deepwater ports licensed under this chapter do not possess the status of islands and have no territorial seas of their own".[16] A US-registered deepwater part is subject to the federal laws of the United States, not as U.S. territory, but rather "as if such port were an area of exclusive Federal jurisdiction located within a State".[17]

The Act also submits foreign ships calling at or utilizing a US-registered deepwater port, but only on the basis of a bilateral agreement with the United States. Lacking such an agreement, the secretary of State shall notify the flag State of the United States' intention to exercise jurisdiction[18]; the flag State is entitled to object, and such objection, apparently, will prevent the exercise of the U.S. jurisdiction (but also prompt the port Authorities to deny entry clearance to the foreign ship involved).

As anticipated above,[19] under the Deepwater Port Act the United States have concluded a number of bilateral treaties in the form of an exchange of letter, by which the other contracting State accepts the U.S. jurisdiction over their ships.[20]

It is significant that the United States have deemed necessary to conclude bilateral agreements with the flag States in order to exercise their jurisdiction over foreign ships using their artificial ports in the high waters.

Moreover, the treaty practice originated by the Deepwater Port Act, while significant, remains quite circumscribed, not only in respect to the number of State involved and the importance of their maritime interests, but also in respect to the

(Footnote 13 continued)

Denmark on the Oresund (United Nations 1993a) bridge does not appear to treat the bridge as national territory of either party, but merely as a good, the issue related to territorial waters being regulated separately (Article 19).

[14]U.S. House of Representatives (2016).

[15]§ 1502(9)(A).

[16]§ 1518(a)(1).

[17]*Ibidem.*

[18]§ 1518(a)(3) and (c).

[19]See Chap. 1.

[20]United Nations (1979a, b, c, d, 1980a, b, 1982, 1983, 1984, 1989, 1993b, 1995a, b, 1998a, b, c, d, e, 2001, 2002a, b).

subject of the international agreements which have been concluded. Indeed, all the international agreement which have been stipulated pursuant to the Deepwater Port Act apply to only one offshore port, the Louisiana Offshore Oil Port (LOOP),[21] and, as the practice related to such treaties has evolved, such limitation has been made explicit in the titles of the treaties.

In conclusion, the State practice related to the US Deepwater Port Act hardly appears to be of much help in order to establish the international legal regime of offshore ports.

## References

Bardin, A. (2002). Coastal state's jurisdiction over foreign vessels. *Pace International law Review, 14*(1), 27ff.

Churchill, R. R., & Lowe, A. V. (1988). *The law of the sea* (II ed.). Manchester: Manchester University Press.

Fietta, S., & Cleverly, R. (2015). *Maritime boundary delimitation.* Oxford: Oxford University Press.

International Court of Justice. (2009). Maritime delimitation in the Black Sea (Romania v. Ukraine). In *I.C.J. Reports*, 2009, pp. 61ff.

International Tribunal for the Law of the Sea. (2003). Case concerning land reclamation by Singapore in and around the Straits of Johor (Malaysia v. Singapore)—Provisional measures—Order of 8 October 2003. *ITLOS Reports*, 2003, p. 10.

International Tribunal for the Law of the Sea. (2015a). *Dispute Concerning the Enrica Lexie Incident—The Italian Republic v. the Republic of India—Request of the Italian Republic for the Prescription of Provisional Measures Under Article 290, Paragraph 5, of the United Nations Convention on the Law of the Sea*, Vol. 1, 21 July 2015.

International Tribunal for the Law of the Sea. (2015b). *The "Enrica Lexie" Incident (Italy v. India)—Request for the prescription of provisional measures—Order*, Year 2015, 24 August 2015.

Kolb, R. (2003). *Case law on equitable maritime delimitation.* The Hague-London-New York: Martinus Nijhoff Publishers.

Lauterpacht, E. (Ed.). (1948). *International law reports.* Cambridge: Cambridge University Press.

Loop LLC. (2016). About Loop. *Loop LCC.* https://www.loopllc.com/About-Loop/Story

Mannucci, G. (2014). *Il conflitto di giurisdizione tra Italia e India nel caso Enrica Lexie.* Florence: Firenze University Press.

Molenaar, E. J. (1998). *Coastal state jurisdiction over vessel-source pollution.* The Hague-Boston-London: Kluwer Law International.

Nordquist, M. H., et al. (1995). *United Nations convention on the law of the sea, 1982: A commentary.* The Hague: Martinus Nijhoof Publishers.

Shalowitz, A. L., & Reed, M. W. (2000). *Shore and sea boundaries* (Vol. 3). Washington: U.S. Printing Office.

Symmons, C. R. (2005). *Selected contemporary issues in the law of the sea.* The Hague: Martinus Nijhoff Publishers.

Tanaka, Y. (2012). *The international law of the sea.* Cambridge: Cambridge University Press.

United Nations. (1979a). Exchange of notes constituting an agreement relating to jurisdiction over vessels in United States deepwater ports. Washington, 27 October 1978 and 15 January 1979. In *United Nations Treaty Series* (Vol. 1153, pp. 283ff).

[21]Loop LLC (2016).

United Nations. (1979b). Exchange of notes constituting an agreement relating to jurisdiction over vessels in United States deepwater ports. Washington, 17 and 22 August 1978. In *United Nations Treaty Series* (Vol. 1153, pp. 145ff).

United Nations. (1979c). Exchange of notes constituting an agreement relating to jurisdiction over vessels in United States deepwater ports. Washington, 11 July 1978. in *United Nations Treaty Series* (Vol. 1153, pp. 89ff).

United Nations. (1979d). Exchange of notes constituting an agreement relating to jurisdiction over vessels in United States deepwater ports. Washington, 17 and 22 August 1978. In *United Nations Treaty Series* (Vol. 1153, pp. 139ff).

United Nations. (1980a). Exchange of notes constituting an agreement concerning the use of the Louisiana Offshore Oil Port (LOOP) by vessels registered in the United Kingdom, the West Indies Associated States or its other territories or flying the flag of the United Kingdom. Washington, 14 and 25 May 1979. In *United Nations Treaty Series* (Vol. 1162, pp. 351ff).

United Nations. (1980b). Exchange of notes constituting an agreement relating to jurisdiction over vessels in United States deepwater ports. Washington, 22 June and 11 July 1979. In *United Nations Treaty Series* (Vol. 1179, pp. 125ff).

United Nations. (1982). Exchange of notes constituting an agreement relating to jurisdiction over vessels in United States deepwater ports. Washington, 15 August and 10 October 1980. In *United Nations Treaty Series* (Vol. 1275, pp. 97ff).

United Nations. (1983). Exchange of notes constituting an agreement concerning the jurisdiction of the United States over Netherlands vessels utilizing the Louisiana Offshore Oil Port (LOOP). Washington, 9 and 16 March 1981. In *United Nations Treaty Series* (Vol. 1307, pp. 409ff).

United Nations. (1984). Exchange of notes constituting an agreement concerning jurisdiction over vessels using the Louisiana Offshore Oil Port (LOOP). Madrid, 5 and 22 November 1983. In *United Nations Treaty Series* (Vol. 1381, pp. 299ff).

United Nations. (1985). Convention on maritime delimitation (with map). Signed at Paris on 16 February 1984. In *United Nations Treaty Series* (Vol. 1411, pp. 289ff).

United Nations. (1989). Exchange of notes constituting an agreement concerning jurisdiction over vessels utilizing the Louisiana Offshore Oil Port. Washington, 2 July 1981 and 4 and 15 September 1981. In *United Nations Treaty Series* (Vol 1534, pp. 111ff).

United Nations (1993a). Agreement on a fixed link over the Sound (with annexes and additional protocol). Signed at Copenhagen on 23 March 1991. In *United Nations Treaty Series* (Vol. 1739, pp. 369ff).

United Nations. (1993b). Exchange of notes constituting an agreement relating to jurisdiction over vessels utilizing the Louisiana Offshore Oil Port. Athens, 7 and 12 May 1982. In *United Nations Treaty Series* (Vol. 1750, pp. 417ff).

United Nations. (1995a). Exchange of notes constituting an agreement relating to jurisdiction over vessels utilizing the Louisiana Offshore Oil Port. Jeddah, 1 March 1981 and 20 October 1982. In *United Nations Treaty Series* (Vol. 1871, pp. 165ff).

United Nations (1995b). Exchange of notes constituting an agreement relating to jurisdiction over vessels utilizing the Louisiana Offshore Oil Port. Washington, 12 and 19 January 1982. In *United Nations Treaty Series* (Vol. 1871, pp. 195ff).

United Nations (1998a). Agreement between the United States of America and Bahamas relating to jurisdiction over vessels utilizing the Louisiana Offshore Oil Port. Nassau, 23 September 1982 and 5 October 1982. In *United Nations Treaty Series* (Vol. 2014, pp. 451ff).

United Nations. (1998b). Agreement between the United States of America and Belgium relating to jurisdiction over vessels utilizing the Louisiana Offshore Oil Port. Washington, 1 and 9 December 1983. In *United Nations Treaty Series* (Vol. 2015, pp. 19ff).

United Nations. (1998c). Agreement between the United States of America and Singapore relating to jurisdiction over vessels utilizing the Louisiana Offshore Oil Port. Singapore, 1 September 1983 and 5 October 1983. In *United Nations Treaty Series* (Vol. 2015, pp. 117ff).

United Nations. (1998d). Exchange of notes constituting an agreement relating to jurisdiction over vessels utilizing the Louisiana Offshore Oil Port. Nicosia, 3 August and 7 September 1983. In *United Nations Treaty Series* (Vol. 2011, pp. 121ff).

United Nations. (1998e). Exchange of notes constituting an agreement relating to jurisdiction over vessels utilizing the Louisiana Offshore Oil Port. Washington, 1 December 1982. In *United Nations Treaty Series* (Vol. 2000, pp. 451ff).

United Nations. (2001). Agreement between the United States of America and Gabon relating to jurisdiction over vessels utilizing the Louisiana Offshore Oil Port. Libreville, 25 July 1984 and 2 August 1984. In *United Nations Treaty Series* (Vol. 2143, pp. 451ff).

United Nations. (2002a). Agreement between the United States of America and Poland relating to jurisdiction over vessels utilizing the Louisiana Offshore Oil Port. Washington, 30 March 1984 and 10 April 1984. In *United Nations Treaty Series* (Vol. 2174, pp. 199ff).

United Nations. (2002b). Agreement between the United States of America and Turkey relating to jurisdiction over vessels utilizing the Louisiana Offshore Oil Port. Washington, 9 and 10 April 1984. In *United Nations Treaty Series* (Vol. 2174, pp. 187ff).

U.S. District Court, S.D. Florida, Miami Division. (2006). Movimento Democracia, Inc., Mercedes Hernandez Guerrero, et al., Plaintiffs, v. Michael Chertoff, Department of Homeland Security, et al., Defendants, No. 06-20044CIV. Order Denying Defendant's Motion for Summary Judgment. In *Federal Supplement, Second Series, 417*, 1343ff.

U.S. House of Representatives. (2016). *United States Code*. Title 33, Chapter 29.

Venice Port Authority. (2010). The Offshore Terminal. *Port of Venice*. https://www.port.venice.it/en/the-offshore-terminal.html

Yang, H. (2006). *Jurisdiction of the coastal state over foreign merchant ships in internal water and the territorial sea*. Berlin-Heidelberg: Springer.

# Part IV
# The Port of Globalization

# Chapter 12
# An Unprecedented Economic Significance and the Ascendance of the Multinational Terminal Operators

US entrepreneur Malcolm McLean is credited with inventing containerization in the Fifties of the XX century. Actually, McLean claimed to have had the idea back in the Thirties, during the Great Depression, when he was working as a truck driver and was frustrated by the dead time of stevedoring.[1] Then he correctly guessed that the movement of goods would have been much rationalized by loading and unloading the whole trailer rather than individual crates. This is still the fundamental principle of multimodal transportation: the box in which the goods are stored should remain sealed from the establishment of the producer to the recipient. This is possible by using a standard container, which can be moved by truck, rail and ship.[2]

Multimodal transportation, in turn, is credited with turning shipping into the "conveyor belt of globalization" as it became widespread in the Seventies of XX century.[3] In 2014, global seaborne shipments increased by 3.4%, reaching a volumes total of 9.84 billion tons.[4] In 1970, the total was 2.53 billion tons.[5]

As for the impact of multimodal transportation over ports, it is commonly said that the use of standard containers allowed to replace the elite dockers and longshoremen with unskilled workers. Actually, the situation is much more complex.

First, as it will be seen further on,[6] traditional port workers still have a relevant role at least in some ports, particularly European ones. Secondly, the new port employees are, rather than unskilled—working on a dock still requires training and experience—, in a much weaker relationship with the port they operate in. Indeed, container standardization has made the knowledge of the docks and berths of a given port, and of the ships and cargoes routinely using it, much less of a necessity:

[1]Mayo and Nohria (2005).
[2]See ISO (2016).
[3]Jung (2005).
[4]UNCTAD (2015), pp. 5ff.
[5]UNCTAD (2016).
[6]Chapter 13.



M. Casagrande, *Seaports in International Law*, SpringerBriefs in Law,
DOI 10.1007/978-3-319-60396-4_12

so much that, sometimes, ships can use their own seafarers as temporary dock workers in the so-called "self-handling". This has had a massive impact, since the close, almost symbiontic relationship between a port and its cohesive corps of port workers used to be a cornerstone of port and port city culture.

However, port workers' organizations were not the only subjects of port clusters involved. The various public Authorities[7] and local private entities taking part to port operations have lost a significant part of their influence and bargaining power to multinational port operators, better known as "terminal operators", since a contemporary port is organized into independent terminals, mostly container terminals.

The standardization of multimodal transportation gives a distinct advantage to a small number of major multinational enterprises, which are able to generate economies of scale and, in some case, even influence sea traffic and routes, being also major shipping companies. According to a list of top port executives drawn up by Lloyd's,[8] between the most important port operators worldwide there are Singapore's PSA International,[9] Hong Kong's Hutchison Port Holdings[10] and China Merchants Holdings International,[11] Netherlands' APM Terminals,[12] United Arab Emirates' DP World,[13] China's COSCO[14] and Shanghai International Port,[15] Philippines' International Container Terminal Services[16] and Turkey's Yilport Holdings.[17]

---

[7]It is commonly assumed that every port is managed by a Port Authority, but the existing practice is much more complex and various. Many ports still have a Harbormaster's Office and/or a Maritime Authority, which can be different than the Port Authority. Port operations are usually also under the concurrent jurisdiction of separate health, border, customs, tax and law enforcement Authorities. Quasi-public functions are often performed by private entities such as the providers of technical-nautical services (towage, pilotage and mooring). Further public or private entities will provide, in regime of public or private law, various services such as railway transportation, ship refueling, cleaning and waste disposal, passenger reception, shipping agency, etc. On the other hand, a number of ports in the same State will sometimes share the same administrative and/or managing Authorities, a prominent case being the Spanish Port System, under which 46 ports are managed by 28 Port Authorities under the jurisdiction of Puertos del Estado, a national State-owned entity (Puertos del Estado 2016).

[8]Lloyd's List (2016).

[9]PSA International (2016a, b).

[10]Hutchison Port Holdings Limited (2016a, b).

[11]China Merchants Holdings (International) Co., Ltd. (2016a, b).

[12]APM Terminals (2016).

[13]DP World (2016a, b).

[14]COSCO Container Lines Co., Ltd. (2016a, b).

[15]Shanghai International Port(Group) Co., Ltd. (2016).

[16]ICTSI (2013a, b).

[17]Yilport Holding Inc. (2016a, b).

In a documents drafted for the Inter-American Committee on Ports,[18] Rossignol adds Taiwan's Evergreen Marine Co.,[19] Germany's EUROGATE[20] and HHLA,[21] and United States' SSA Marine.[22]

Finally, Denmark's Maersk[23] is a major shipping and port operator, the history of which dates back to 1918.[24]

The list of the most important multinational port operators, incidentally, shows the shift Eastwards in the balance of maritime commerce power. Indeed, according to the World Shipping Council, in 2013 nine in ten of the most important container ports in the world were located in Asia.[25]

## References


Møller-Maersk, A. P. A/S. (2016a). Our history. *Maersk*. http://www.maersk.com/en/the-maersk-group/about-us#company-structure

Møller-Maersk, A. P. A/S. (2016b). Operation in wartime. *Maersk*. http://www.maersk.com/en/hardware/fleet/events/operation-in-wartime

APM Terminals. (2016). Company information. *APM Terminals*. http://www.apmterminals.com/en/about-us/company-information

China Merchants Holdings (International) Co., Ltd. (2016a). Company profile. *China Merchants Holdings (International) Company Limited*. http://www.cmhi.com.hk/Catalog_31.aspx

China Merchants Holdings (International) Co., Ltd. (2016b). History. *China Merchants Holdings (International) Company Limited*. http://www.cmhi.com.hk/Catalog_31.aspx

COSCO Container Lines Co., Ltd. (2016a). Company profile. *COSCO Websites*. http://www.coscon.com/layouts/aboutUsLayout.jsp?page=company

COSCO Container Lines Co., Ltd. (2016b). Memorabilia. *COSCO Websites*. http://www.coscon.com/aboutUs/toMemorabilia.do?page=memorabiliaIndex&bilingual=1

DP World. (2016a). About DP world. *DP World*. http://web.dpworld.com/about-dp-world/

DP World. (2016b). Our journey. *DP World*. http://web.dpworld.com/about-dp-world/our-journey/

EUROGATE GmbH & Co. KGaA, KG. (2016a). EUROGATE – Moving the global economy. *EUROGATE*. http://www1.eurogate.de/en/About-us/What-we-do

EUROGATE GmbH & Co. KGaA, KG. (2016b). Corporate history of EUROGATE. *EUROGATE*. http://www1.eurogate.de/en/About-us/History

Evergreen Marine Corp. (2016). Corporate profile. Evergreen Marine Corp. http://www.evergreen-marine.com/tbi1/jsp/TBI1_CorporateProfile.jsp


[18]See Chap. 10.

[19]Evergreen Marine Corp. (2016).

[20]EUROGATE GmbH & Co. KGaA, KG (2016a, b).

[21]Hamburger Hafen und Logistik AG (2016a, b).

[22]SSA Marine (2016a, b).

[23]A.P. Møller-Maersk A/S (2016a).

[24]During World War II, the company temporarily relocated to the United States, putting at the disposal of the U.S. Government a fleet of 36 large ships: A.P. Møller-Maersk A/S (2016b).

[25]World Shipping Council (2016). The ten ports are, in order of importance: Shanghai, Singapore, Shenzhen, Hong Kong, Busan, Ningbo-Zhoushan, Qingdao, Guangzhou, Jebel Ali and Tianjin. Since Jebel Ali is in the United Arab Emirates, not a single European or American port is listed.

Hamburger Hafen und Logistik AG. (2016a). Hamburger Hafen und Logistik AG. *HHLA*. http://hhla.de/en/group.html

Hamburger Hafen und Logistik AG. (2016b). HHLA history. *HHLA*. http://hhla.de/en/history/overview.html

Hutchison Port Holdings Limited. (2016a). Company profile. *HPH*. https://www.hph.com/en/webpg-87.html.

Hutchison Port Holdings Limited. (2016b). Milestones. *HPH*. https://www.hph.com/en/about/milestone.html

ICTSI. (2013a). About us. *International Container Terminal Services, Inc.* http://www.ictsi.com/content/about-us/about-us/

ICTSI. (2013b). Timeline. *International Container Terminal Services, Inc.* http://www.ictsi.com/content/about-us/timeline/

ISO. (2016). Standards catalogue. *ISO*, 55.180.10: General purpose containers. http://www.iso.org/iso/home/store/catalogue_ics.htm

Jung, A. (2005). The box that makes the world go round. *Spiegel Online*, 25 November 2005.

Lloyd's List. (2016). Top 10 box port heavyweights. *Lloyd's List*. https://www.lloydslist.com/ll/news/top100/ports-and-logistics/

Mayo, A. J., & Nohria, N. (2005). The truck driver who reinvented shipping. In *Working knowledge*, 3 October 2005.

PSA International. (2016a). About Us. *PSA*. https://www.globalpsa.com/#homeOurMission

PSA International. (2016b). Heritage. *PSA*. https://www.globalpsa.com/heritage/

Puertos del Estado. (2016). About us. *Puertos del Estado*. http://www.puertos.es/en-us/nosotrospuertos/Pages/Nosotros.aspx

Shanghai International Port(Group) Co., Ltd. (2016). About Port of Shanghai. *SIPG*. http://www.portshanghai.com.cn/en/channel1/channel11.html

SSA Marine. (2016a). Overview. *SSA Marine*. http://www.ssamarine.com/company/overview.html

SSA Marine. (2016b). History. *SSA Marine*. http://www.ssamarine.com/company/history.html

UNCTAD. (2016). World seaborne trade by types of cargo and country groups, annual, 1970-2014. *UNCTADstat*. http://unctadstat.unctad.org/wds/TableViewer/tableView.aspx?ReportId=32363

UNCTAD. (2015). *Review of Maritime Transport 2015*. United Nations Publication.

World Shipping Council. (2016). Top 50 world container ports. *World Shipping Council*. http://www.worldshipping.org/about-the-industry/global-trade/top-50-world-container-ports

Yilport Holding Inc. (2016a). Yildirim group. *Yilport Holding Inc.* http://www.yilport.com/sayfa.asp?mdl=sayfalar&id=1

Yilport Holding Inc. (2016b). Milestones. *Yilport Holding Inc.* http://www.yilport.com/sayfa.asp?mdl=sayfalar&id=2

# Chapter 13
# The Decline of the Longshoremen's Organizations and Their Resistance in Europe

It is a common assumption that traditional dock work was erased, or at least is being phased out, by containerization.[1] The situation is actually more complex and nuanced, at least in Europe, where port workers' organizations have a long tradition, just like the traditional port communities of which they are part.[2]

Indeed, such communities have proven their ability to lobby the European Institutions into suspending the process of reforming the European regulation of port governance and services.

As it is often the case at the European level, such process was started in 1991 by the Court of Justice with the famous judgment on the port of Genoa case,[3] when the Court declared the incompatibility with EU law of the Italian legislation granting to the Italian port workers' organizations ("compagnie portuali") a monopoly over stevedoring services. The impact of the judgment was such that Italy had to overhaul its entire port legislation.[4]

In 1997, however, the European Commission noted that port monopolies were surviving outside Italy.[5] In an attempt to extend a harmonized regime to the whole Internal Market, in 2002 the Commission presented what became known as "Ports Package I," a proposal of Directive,[6] which was rejected by the European Parliament in 2003. A watered-down "Ports Package II"[7] had the same fate in

[1]Blok and Downey (2003), p. 100.
[2]The entry into a port market by a multinational port operator, indeed, will damage not only the dock workers, but most local port operators. The latter, due to their small dimensions, will be unable to compete against the newcomer, which is also likely to challenge the local legislation and practice protecting the traditional operators. A typical example is a small, local terminal operator, which was granted by the Port Authority a long term exclusive concession, often paying outdated, very low concession fees.
[3]European Court of Justice (1991). See Guéguen-Hallouët (2003), Maresca (2001), p. 39ff.
[4]State Printing Service and Mint (1994).
[5]European Commission (1997a), p. 27.
[6]European Commission (2002).
[7]European Commission (2004).



M. Casagrande, *Seaports in International Law*, SpringerBriefs in Law,
DOI 10.1007/978-3-319-60396-4_13

2006.[8] During the debate on the first Package, port workers from all over Europe put the European Parliament under siege, so much that the seat of Strasbourg was surrounded by the French Army[9]; the debate indeed shows that the complaints by the port workers played a significant part in the rejection of the Package.

After the activism shown in the port of Genoa case, the action of the European Institutions became more timid.

On one hand, the Commission and the Court of Justice did not hesitate to censure unreasonably high or discriminatory port dues.[10]

On the other hand, in the same lapse of time, the European Court of Justice ruled that activities related to the prevention of port pollution are exempt from the application of EU competition law,[11] and the European Commission ruled that EU State aid law is not applicable to the towage fleet of the port of Venice, since it operates at the local level in a sector which was not liberalized.[12] Since the green port is a universally recognized policy priority, it is easy to understand that the last judgment by the Court of Justice has wide-ranging implications.[13] The Commission Decision on the port of Venice is also puzzling, at least insofar as it downplays the importance of the market of technical-nautical services in the said port. Venice might not be a major container port, also due to the delicate geography of its Lagoon, but it is a very important cruise port.[14] Moreover, within the port of Venice—again, due to the peculiarities and the low depth of the Lagoon—towage is compulsory for ships.[15]

The Parliament, by its part, appears unambiguously supporting the traditional status quo in seaports: between 2007 and 2008, the Commission accepted not to interfere in the port sector with hard law norms, and the Parliament welcomed such pledge.[16]

The practical results of this resistance by the European traditional port communities against the new port governance models is some sort of hybrid regime, in which various degrees of liberalization coexist with the survival of regulated market segments and protected operators.[17] In some extreme examples, such as the Athens port of Piraeus, the old and new regime can coexist on contiguous docks. In 2009, indeed, COSCO was granted a concession over some docks,[18] while other have remained under the influence of the local port workers' organizations, which are

[8]This time the proposal of a Directive was withdrawn by the Commission.

[9]European Parliament (2003).

[10]European Court of Justice (1994, 1997a, 1997b, 2010).

[11]European Court of Justice (1997b).

[12]European Commission (2000).

[13]ESPO (2012).

[14]Venice Port Authority (2010).

[15]Venice Harbormaster's Office (2012).

[16]European Commission (2007), European Parliament (2008).

[17]Van Hooydonk (2013).

[18]Barnard (2010), China COSCO Holdings Company Limited (2009).

exceptionally entrenched[19] and have predictably started a furious campaign against the Chinese newcomers.[20] In 2016, thanks to the privatization campaign started by the Greek Government under pressure by the international creditors, COSCO was able to acquire a majority stake in the whole port".[21]

Beside the very peculiar Greek case, the European Commission for some years has appeared willing to reopen the seaports file, with the presentation of a new Ports Package,[22] the legislative iter of which has been, however, troubled. On 8 March 2016 the Draft Regulation was discussed and heavily amended by the European Parliament, with rapporteur Knut Fleckenstein defending port specificity and the Parliament's decision to "dismiss the forced free market access to port services."[23]

Meanwhile, the Commission, exercising its wide discretionary powers in the field of State aid, amended the General Block Exemption Regulation in order to include, inter alia, State aid to seaports. Interestingly, the amendment included in the GBER a legal definition of port as "an area of land and water made up of infrastructure and equipment for, principally, the reception of waterborne vessels, their loading and unloading, the storage of goods, the receipt and delivery of those goods, or the embarkation and disembarkation of passengers and any other infrastructure necessary for transport operators within the port area."[24]

More generally, EU law, despite many political hurdles, has shown more focus on seaports than international law, probably due to its free market orientation, which sooner or later was bound to collide with the very closed markets of local port clusters. One can also speculate that some lobbying by multinational port operators and shipping companies, together with the strategic economic significance of ports and the anachronistic privileged vested in some traditional port

[19]Barnard (2009), Lim (2011) and Malkoutzis (2011). As further evidence of how much intertwined dockers' organizations can be with the local Authorities, in 2009 the Prefect of Piraeus lodged a complaint with the European Commission over alleged State aid granted by his own Government to COSCO. The complaint was dismissed in 2012 (European Commission 2012).

[20]Wikileaks made public a 2008 cablo of the U.S. Embassy in Athens, in which the Piraeus dockworkers' organizations are depicted as a parasitic clique: "The Dockworkers' Union and the Federation of Greek Port Personnel have long held a labor monopoly over the operations of Greece's two major ports in Piraeus and in Thessaloniki. Controlling exclusive contracts with the Piraeus Port Authority (OLP), the unions have reaped substantial financial benefits, with ironclad job security, guaranteed hiring privileges for the children of union members, and annual dockworker salaries in the range of 90.000–140.000 euro (135.000–210.000 USD), once overtime and other benefits are factored in—far above the average Greek yearly salary of 32.280 USD (National Statistics Services of Greece, data for 2008). According to union contacts, EBEA, and media reports, dockworkers also benefit from systematized corruption, manipulating the customs processing bureaucracy to expedite the containers of shippers who pay an extra fee—or holding up imports for those who refuse. All of this translates into what EBEA describes as the most expensive port in Europe in terms of fees and costs for shipping companies, importers, and exporters" (Wikileaks 2016).

[21]Stamouli (2016).

[22]European Council (2013).

[23]European Parliament (2016).

[24]European Commission (2015), Article 1(2).

operators, played a role in encouraging this partial activism. Whatever the cause, the—albeit limited—progressive features of EU port law should be treasured. In the last Part of this treatise,[25] an evaluation will be made of the possibility to using the most advanced norms on seaports found in EU and municipal law as a tool to reinterpret and advance the corresponding international regulation.

## References

Barnard, B. (2009). Greek Court Outlaws Piraeus Strike. *Journal of Commerce*, 11 November 2009.

Barnard, B. (2010). Piraeus Terminal Boosts Cosco Pacific Revenue. *Journal of Commerce*, 24 August 2010.

Blok, A., & Downey, G. (2003). *Uncovering labour in information revolutions, 1750–2000*. Cambdrige: Cambridge University Press.

China COSCO Holdings Company Limited. (2009). COSCO Pacific Commenced 35-Year Concession in Relation to Piers 2 and 3 of Piraeus Port. Retrieved from: http://en.chinacosco.com/art/2009/10/9/art_1076_35540.html

ESPO. (2012). *ESPO Green Guide*. Brussels: European Sea Ports Organisation-ESPO.

European Commission. (2015). *COMMISSION REGULATION (EU) …/… of XXX amending Regulation (EU) No 651/2014 declaring certain categories of aid compatible with the internal market in application of Articles 107 and 108 of the Treaty – DRAFT*. Retrieved from: http://ec.europa.eu/competition/consultations/2016_gber_review/draft_regulation_en.pdf

European Commission. (2012). *State aid SA.28876 (2012/C) (ex 2011/N) (ex CP 202/2009) – Greece Container Terminal Port of Piraeus & Cosco Pacific Limited*. COM(2012) 4217 final.

European Commission. (2007). *Commission staff working document—Accompanying document to the Communication from the Commission on a European ports policy —Summary impact assessment*. COM(2007) 616 final.

European Commission. (2004). *Proposal for a Directive of the European Parliament and of the Council on Market Access to Port Services*. COM(2004) 0654 final.

European Commission. (2002). *Amended proposal for a Directive of the European Parliament and of the Council On Market Access to Port Services (Presented by the Commission pursuant to Article 250(2) of the EC Treaty)*. COM/2002/0101 final.

European Commission. (2000). Commission Decision of 29 December 1999 on aid to firms in Venice and Chioggia by way of relief from social security contributions under Laws Nos 30/1997 and 206/1995, *Official Journal of the European Union*, n. L150 of 23 June 2000, pp. 50ff.

European Commission. (1997a). *Green paper on sea ports and maritime infrastracture*. Luxembourg: Office for Official Publications.

European Commission. (1997b). Commission Decision of 21 October 1997 relating to a proceeding pursuant to Article 90 (3) of the EC Treaty regarding the tariffs for piloting in the Port of Genoa. *Official Journal of the European Union*, n. L 301 of 5 November 1997, pp. 27ff.

European Council. (2013). *Proposal for a REGULATION OF THE EUROPEAN PARLIAMENT AND OF THE COUNCIL establishing a framework on market access to port services and financial transparency of ports (First reading)*. 2013/0157(COD).

[25]Chapters 18–20.

European Court of Justice. (2010). Arrêt de la Cour (septième chambre), 4 février 2010, Dans l'affaire C-18/09, Commission européenne contre Royaume d'Espagne. *InfoCuria*. Retrieved from: http://curia.europa.eu/juris/document/document.jsf?text=&docid=74926&pageIndex=0&doclang=FR&mode=req&dir=&occ=first&part=1&cid=365419

European Court of Justice. (1997a). Judgement of the Court (Sixth Chamber), 17 July 1997, In Case C-242/95, GT-Link A/S and De Danske Statsbaner (DSB). *InfoCuria*. Retrieved from: http://curia.europa.eu/juris/document/document.jsf?text=&docid=43719&pageIndex=0&doclang=EN&mode=lst&dir=&occ=first&part=1&cid=376584

European Court of Justice. (1997b). Judgment of the Court, 18 March 1997, In Case C-343/95, Diego Calì & Figli Srl and Servizi Ecologici Porto di Genova SpA (SEPG). *European Court Reports*, 1997, pp. I-1580ff.

European Court of Justice. (1994). Judgment of the Court, 17 May 1994, In Case C-18/93, Corsica Ferries Italia Srl and Corpo dei Piloti del Porto di Genova. *European Court Reports*, 1994, pp. I-1812ff.

European Court of Justice. (1991). Judgment of the Court, 10 December 1991, In Case C-179/90, Merci convenzionali porto di Genova SpA and Siderurgica Gabrielli SpA. *European Court Reports*, 1991, pp. I-05889ff.

European Parliament. (2003). Debates: Monday, 10 March 2003, Strasbourg. *European Parliament*. Retrieved from: http://www.europarl.europa.eu/sides/getDoc.do?pubRef=-//EP//TEXT+CRE+20030310+ITEMS+DOC+XML+V0//EN&language=EN#top

European Parliament. (2008). European Parliament resolution of 4 September 2008 on a European ports policy (2008/2007(INI)). *Official Journal of the European Union*, n. C295E of 4 December 2009, pp. 74ff.

European Parliament. (2016). *Port services: improving efficiency to boost trade*. Press release 8 March 2016, 13:15.

Guéguen-Hallouët, G. (2003). Le juge communautaire et l'application des règles de concurrence aux ports maritimes. In Cudennec, A. et al. (Ed.), *Le juge communautaire et la mer*. Brussels: Bruylant, pp. 23ff.

Lim, L. (2011). In Greek Port, Storm Brews Over Chinese-Run Labor. *NPR*, 8 June 2011, Morning Edition.

Malkoutzis, N. (2010). Waiting for the great leap forward. *InsideGreece*, 24 September 2010.

Maresca, M. (2001). *La regolazione dei porti tra diritto interno e diritto comunitario*. Turin: Giappichelli.

Stamouli, N. (2016). Greece Signs Deal to Sell Stake in Port of Piraeus to China's Cosco. *The Wall Street Journal*, 8 April 2016.

State Printing Service and Mint. (1994). Legge 18 gennaio 1994, n. 84. *Gazzetta Ufficiale della Repubblica Italiana*, 4 February 1994, n. 28.

Van Hooydonk, E. (2013). *Port Labour in the EU*, Volume I, Study commissioned by the European Commission, Brussels, Contract Number MOVE/C2/2010-81/SI2.588013, Final Report, 8 January 2013.

Venice Harbormaster's Office. (2012). *Ordinanza n. 155/10*, 31 December 2010.

Venice Port Authority. (2010). Cruises. *Port of Venice*. Retrieved from: https://www.port.venice.it/en/cruises.html

WikiLeaks (2016). Greece: Government manages to suspend port strike, but for how long and at what cost? *WikiLeaks*. Retrieved from: https://wikileaks.org/plusd/cables/09ATHENS1581_a.html

# Chapter 14
# Flags of Convenience and Port State Control

Globalization had a strong impact not only on seaports, but also on national merchant fleets. As anticipated above,[1] the latter used to have a very strong link with their flag State. Such link was ensured by various factors: masters and crewmen being mostly citizens of the flag States, under a special legal status emphasizing their duty of loyalty to the flag State; wide-ranging State powers attributed to the commander and to the consular officials of the flag State; ships being mostly owned and operated by citizens of the flag State, through corporations incorporated under the law of the flag State and having their seat in the flag State.

Almost all these factors have now ceased. Legally, the broken link between ship and flag State is embodied by the widespread practice of the flags of convenience. The maritime legislation of many States has been amended in order to allow ships to be registered in the ship registers of those States—and thus fly their flag—even in the absence of any meaningful link between such ships and the State. This policy was adopted in order to collect from the shipping companies the registration dues and some taxes, although States keeping convenience registers usually offer shipping companies a very advantageous tax regime. In sum, it is a policy very similar to those adopted by tax havens in order to attract corporations.

Convenience registers are usually kept by very small States in order to finance themselves, but also by bigger and richer States—sometimes with a strong maritime

---

[1] Chapter 3.



M. Casagrande, *Seaports in International Law*, SpringerBriefs in Law,
DOI 10.1007/978-3-319-60396-4_14

tradition—, in addition to their traditional register, in order to collect some revenues and avoid losing all the ships flying their flag.[2]

Flags of convenience are not only a problem of tax elusion. The Montego Bay Convention[3] attributes to the flag State the duty to "take such measures for ships flying its flag as are necessary to ensure safety at sea," with regards to their construction, manning, and seaworthiness, but also to the training and the labor conditions of the crews,[4] and also to "ensure compliance by vessels flying their flag or of their registry with applicable international rules and standards."[5] As seen above,[6] in the international law and practice the relation between a State and a ship flying its flag tends to be considered as almost exclusive, and such exclusiveness is strongly defended. Thus, it is still commonly assumed that the responsibility to ensure compliance with international law and standards by a ship rest primarily with the flag State.[7]

It is obvious, however, that very small States or territories such as Tonga do not even have the means, even if they had the political will, to inspect hundreds or thousands of ships.[8]

The problem of ship safety, however, goes beyond the flags of convenience practice. After all, flag States—including the ones with traditional registers—have traditionally delegated ship inspections to recognized and certified private operators, which are widely known as survey and certification companies, but are today officially classified by IMO as Recognized Organizations/Recognized Security Organizations.[9] The services offered by these companies, which often have a long tradition in their field, can be used even by the smallest flag State, since the relevant costs will be sustained by the shipping companies. Unsurprisingly, most State keeping convenience registers were able to react to international pressure by significantly improving their control performance. Indeed, the 2015/2016 flag State

[2]The International Transport Workers' Federation, a major transnational trade union which is very active in the maritime and port sectors, lists as States and territories keeping convenience registers Antigua and Barbuda, Bahamas, Barbados, Belize, Bermuda, Bolivia, Burma, Cambodia, Cayman Islands, Comoros, Cyprus, Equatorial Guinea, Georgia, Gibraltar, Honduras, Jamaica, Lebanon, Liberia, Malta, Marshall Islands, Mauritius, Mongolia, Netherlands Antilles, North Korea, Panama, Sao Tome and Principe, Sri Lanka, St Vincent and the Grenadines, Tonga and Vanuatu, but also Germany and France for their additional registers (International Transport Workers' Federation 2016). The most well-known convenience registers are the Panama (BBC 2014) and the Liberia one (LISCR 2016).

[3]See Chap. 11.

[4]Art. 94, par. 3–4.

[5]Art. 247, par. 1.

[6]Chapter 8.

[7]Dotinga and Kwiatkowska (editors) (2001), p. 40; FAO (2002), Chap. 4; Sands (2012), p. 410; Zwinge (2011).

[8]The Panama Maritime Authority claims that "the Panama Registry is in charge of managing the world's largest ship registry, with over 8000 registered vessels which accounts for 218 million GT [gross tonns], representing 18% of the world fleet" (Panama Maritime Authority 2015).

[9]International Maritime Organization (2016).

performance table published by the International Chamber of Shipping[10] shows, for example, a decent performance by Panama and a spotless one by Liberia; these are the two countries keeping the most important and well-known "open registers." Some of the worst performances are by flag States which are not blacklisted as flag of conveniences such as Costa Rica, the Democratic Republic of Congo, Ivory Coast, and Tanzania.

It is safe to say that, nowadays, to register a ship or a fleet in a convenience register is a matter of tax expedience, rather than of avoiding the enforcement of international standards. The real issue is that flag State control alone has proven unable to effectively monitor the condition of ships traveling over the world's seas.

The issue was progressively raised by a string of very serious accidents involving oil tankers off the European coasts, with the ensuing oil spills and heavy environmental damage.[11]

In reaction, in 1982 fourteen European States[12] concluded the Paris Memorandum of Understanding on Port State Control.[13] The Paris MoU was adopted by IMO as a model,[14] and it served as such for a string of similar agreements which were stipulated after it: the 1992 Viña del Mar Agreement,[15] the 1993 Tokyo MoU,[16] the 1996 Caribbean MoU,[17] the 1997 Mediterranean MoU,[18] the

[10]International Chamber of Shipping (2016).

[11]The tanker Amoco Cadiz ran aground off the coast of Britanny on March 16, 1978 (The International Tankers Owners Pollution Federation Limited 2014). Brittany was so unlucky to be affected also by the sinking of the tanker Erika on December 12, 1999 (Euronews 2012). Finally, the tanker prestige sank off the Spanish Bay of Biscay on November 19, 2002 (BBC 2002). All the three ships were flying a flag of convenience, and the Erika had also been certified by the prestigious Italian corporation RINA (RINA Services s.p.a., 2016), despite its old age (Chrisafis 2008).

[12]Belgium, Denmark, Finland, France, Greece, Ireland, Italy, Netherlands, Norway, Portugal, Spain, Sweden, United Kingdom West Germany. Since 1991 Bulgaria, Canada, Croatia, Croatia, Cyprus, Estonia, Iceland, Latvia, Lithuania, Malta, Romania, Russia, and Slovenia also adhered.

[13]Paris MoU (2016a).

[14]International Maritime Organization (1991).

[15]Argentine Naval Prefecture (2012). The Parties to the Viña del Mar Agreement are Argentina, Bolivia, Brazil, Chile, Colombia, Cuba, the Dominican Republic, Ecuador, Guatemala, Honduras, Mexico, Panama, Peru, Uruguay, and Venezuela.

[16]Tokyo MOU (2016). The Parties to the Tokyo MoU are Australia, Canada, Chile, China (including Hong Kong), Fiji, Indonesia, Japan, Malaysia, Marshall Islands, New Zealand, Papua New Guinea, Peru, Philippines, Russia, Singapore, Solomon Islands, Thailand, South Korea, Vanuatu, and Vietnam. Given the traffic volumes of the Asian seaports (see above, Chap. 11), the Tokyo MoU is probably the most important one in practical terms.

[17]CMOU (2010). The Parties to the Caribbean MoU are Anguilla, Antigua and Barbuda, Aruba, the Bahamas, the Barbados, Belize, Cuba, Bermuda, Dominica, Great Britain (for the British Virgin Islands and the Cayman Islands), Grenada, Guyana, Jamaica, Montserrat, the Netherlands (including Curaçao), Saint Kitts and Nevis, Saint Lucia, Saint Vincent and the Grenadines, Suriname, Trinidad and Tobago, and the Turks and Caicos Islands.

[18]Mediterranean MoU (2014). The Parties to the Mediterranean MoU are Algeria, Cyprus, Egypt, Israel, Jordan, Lebanon, Malta, Morocco, Tunisia, Turkey and the Organization for the Liberation of Palestine (as Palestinian Authority).

1998 Indian Ocean MoU,[19] the 1999 Abuja MoU,[20] the 2000 Black Sea MoU[21] and the 2004 Riyadh MoU.[22] There is not a Port State Control MoU for North America, because the United States has unilaterally adopted their own PSC program[23]; Canada is a member of the Paris MoU, as well as of the Tokyo MoU.

All the MoUs are strikingly similar in their structure and their provisions.

First of all, none of them has been filed for registration in the United Nation Secretariat, the only text available being the ones uploaded on the respective Secretariat websites. All the MoUs were concluded by the unnamed "Maritime Authorities" of the Party States, without a hint of the name or the qualification of the signer, which is incongruous even for the practice of executive agreements.[24] It appears something like an attempt to configure the PSC MoUs as an internum corporis of the maritime community, as if it only the consent of such community could justify the interference of the port State with ships flying a foreign a flag. The latter interference is an exercise of jurisdiction which, despite being perfectly in compliance with international law, at least when triggered by the violation of an international standard by the ship,[25] is usually considered a violation of international comity,[26] or at least of international practice.[27]

Significantly, all MoU also have a preamble in which the primary jurisdiction of the flag State over its ships, including their compliance with international standards, is reaffirmed, before adding that a contribution by port States is nevertheless needed.

After the preamble, in each MoU will be found, approximately in this order, a commitment by the Parties to exercise their port State jurisdiction pursuant to the

---

[19]Indian Ocean Memorandum of Understanding on Port State Control (2014).

[20]Abuja MoU (2012). The Parties to the Abuja MoU are Angola, Benin, Cameroon, Cape Verde, Congo, the Democratic Republic of Congo, Equatorial Guinea, Gabon, the Gambia, Ghana, Guinea, Guinea Bissau, the Ivory Coast, Liberia, Mauritania, Namibia, Nigeria, Sao Tome and Principe, Sierra Leone, Senegal, South Africa, and Togo.

[21]Black Sea MOU (2016). The Parties to the Black Sea MoU are Bulgaria, Georgia, Romania, Russia, Turkey, and Ukraine.

[22]Riyadh MoU on PSC (2015). The Parties to the Riyadh MoU are Bahrain, Oman, Qatar, Saudi Arabia, United Arab Emirates, and Kuwait.

[23]United States Coast Guard (2016).

[24]Setting aside all the other oddities detected in PSC MoUs, the prevailing doctrine holds that executive agreements are pleno jure international agreements, which should be registered with the United Nations: Brandon (1953), p. 52; Elias (1974), pp. 222ff.; McNair (1961), p. 181, albeit with some limitations; Rosenne (1970), pp. 402ff.

[25]See Chap. 11.

[26]The issue of the exact nature and definition of international comity—a term which is used with very different meaning, some of which related to private international law—cannot be dealt with here.

[27]Churchill and Lowe (1993), p. 80; Dunlap (1996), p. 14; Kasoulides (1993), p. 25; Molenaar (1998), p. 193; Ozcayir (2004), pp. 86ff; Quadri (1939), p. 91; Treves (1995), p. 38.

MoU,[28] a list of the international standards covered by the MoU,[29] the criteria to select the ships to inspect,[30] the sanctions to be applied to the ships found not in compliance with the standards (namely, the detention of the ship[31] and, more rarely, her ban from the ports covered by the MoU[32]), the establishment of a Secretariat to supervise and coordinate the execution of the MoU,[33] and finally the procedures to be used to amend the MoU,[34] followed by technical Annexes.

Since every Secretariat maintains a free access database of its inspections and detentions, it is possible to assess the effectiveness of each regional PSC system. The result is a mixed picture.[35] In 2015, under the Paris MoU were made 17,858 inspections and 41,436 deficiencies were detected in 9381 ships, 595 of which were detained. In the same year, under the Tokyo MoU, covering very busy sea lanes, 42,442 inspections were made, leading to the detention of 1153 ships. The Abuja MoU Secretariat database does not offer numerical outputs, so the 2014 report by the Secretariat was used; according to that source,[36] in 2013 2916 inspections were made, which led to the detection of 609 deficiencies and the detention of 14 ships: not much, for a high-risk area like Africa. However, the most striking results come from the Riyadh MoU, covering an area crowded with oil tankers, the very type of ship which led to the adoption of the regional PSC regimes. In 2015, under this MoU just 30 inspection (29 of which in Bahrain) were made; the said inspections led to the detention of 5 ships.

[28]Section 1 of the Paris MoU; Section 1 of the Viña del Mar Agreement; Section 1 of the Tokyo MoU; Section 1 of the Caribbean MoU; Section 1 of the Mediterranean MoU; Section 1 of the Abuya MoU; Section 1 of the Black Sea MoU; Section 1 of the Riyadh MoU.

[29]Section 2 of the Paris MoU; Section 2 of the Viña del Mar Agreement; Section 2 of the Tokyo MoU; Section 2 of the Caribbean MoU; Section 2 of the Mediterranean MoU; Section 2 of the Abuya MoU; Section 2 of the Black Sea MoU; Section 2 of the Riyadh MoU.

[30]Section 3 of the Paris MoU; Section 3 of the Viña del Mar Agreement; Section 3.3ff. of the Tokyo MoU; Section 3 of the Caribbean MoU; Section 3 of the Mediterranean MoU; Section 3 of the Abuja MoU; Section 3 of the Black Sea MoU; Section 3 of the Riyadh MoU.

[31]Section 3.4ff. of the Paris MoU; Section 3.10ff. of the Viña del Mar Agreement; Section 3.7ff. of the Tokyo MoU; Section 3.7.1ff. of the Caribbean MoU; Section 3.6.3ff. of the Mediterrean MoU; Section 3.4.3 of the Abuja MoU; Section 3.6.4ff. of the Black Sea MoU; Section 3.14ff. of the Riyadh MoU.

[32]Section 4 of the Paris MoU; Section 4 of the Abuja MoU.

[33]Section 7 of the Paris MoU; Section 6 of the Viña del Mar Agreement; Section 6 of the Tokyo MoU; Section 6 of the Caribbean MoU; Section 6 of the Mediterranean MoU; Section 8 of the Abuja MoU; Section 7 of the Black Sea MoU; Section 7 of the Riyadh MoU.

[34]Section 8 of the Paris MoU; Section 7 of the Viña del Mar Agreement; Section 7 of the Tokyo MoU; Section 8 of the Caribbean MoU; Section 7 of the Mediterranean MoU; Section 10 of the Abuja MoU; Section 9 of the Black Sea MoU; Section 9 of the Riyadh MoU. Most MoU have been amended, especially in their Technical Annexes.

[35]Bang (2008).

[36]Abuja MoU (2012).

Yet, according to the Safety & Shipping Review 2016,[37] since 2006 the losses of ships have been steadily decreasing all over the world, from a peak of 171 in 2007 to 85 in 2015.[38] Regionally, the losses are concentrated in the Far East,[39] where ports and sea lanes are more busy. It is clearly not a matter of port State control, since, according to the data, the regime operating under the Tokyo MoU is quite effective.

A possible reason is that the decrease in the number of serious maritime accidents is due to efforts made by flag States, rather than by the establishment of port State control regimes. However, the apparently modest impact of PSC could indicate that the data found in the Secretariats' databases are misleading.

First of all, they should be compared with the traffic data of the seaports covered by the relevant PSC regime. In 2015, 29,122 ships called at the port of Rotterdam alone,[40] thus making the 17,858 inspections made under the Paris MoU a less impressive number. In the same year, 29,011 ships called at the port of Hong Kong,[41] covered by the Tokyo MoU, under which 42,442 inspection were conducted.

Moreover, PSC regimes are always based on the clear grounds rule.[42] Under the rule, the officer conducting the inspection (Port State Control Officer-PSCO) will normally have to restrict himself to a prima facie review of the ship, moving on to a detailed inspection only if he finds that there are clear grounds for believing that the vessel is not in compliance with a relevant international standard. Moreover, clear grounds are analytically detailed in each MoU, even if the list is not binding on the PSCO. In practice, the detailed inspection will take place only if the ship is unable to present the required papers and certification, or if it is affected by a self-evident deficiency.

Finally, the detention of a ship is treated in all MoUs as an extrema ratio measure, and the ban—id est the denial of access to seaports—is contemplated only in the Paris and Abuja MoUs. In most cases, the ship will simply be ordered to remove the deficiencies detected by the inspection; even if it detained, the detention will be lifted as soon as the ship is judged to be seaworthy again. A very cautious approach, which is also clearly visible in the Code of Good Practices for Port State Control Officers adopted in the framework of the Paris MoU.[43] There, the PSCO is

---

[37]Allianz Global Corporate & Specialty SE (2016).

[38]Allianz Global Corporate & Specialty SE (2016), p. 4.

[39]Allianz Global Corporate & Specialty SE (2016), p. 5.

[40]Port of Rotterdam (2016).

[41]Hong Kong Special Administrative Region (2016).

[42]Annex 9, n. 3 of the Paris MoU; Annex 1, n. 2.4 of the Viña del Mar Agreement; Section 3.1 of the Tokyo MoU; Section 3.1 of the Caribbean MoU; Section 3.2.1 of the Mediterranean MoU; Section 3.3 of the Abuja MoU; Section 3.1.2 of the Black Sea MoU; Section 3.2 of the Riyadh MoU. It is significant that the clear grounds rule, which is found only in the Annexes of the Paris MoU, was moved to the main text in all the subsequent instruments, as if the need was felt to emphasize its importance as a guarantee for the ship.

[43]Paris MoU (2016b).

instructed to "remember that a ship is a home as well as a workplace for the ship's personnel and not unduly disturb their rest or privacy,"[44] "comply with any ship housekeeping rules such as removing dirty shoes or work clothes,"[45] "respect the authority of the Master or his deputy,"[46] "comply with all security requirements of the ship and wait to be escorted around the ship by a responsible person."[47] In 28 paragraphs, at least 16 are focused on the duties of the PSCO toward the master and the crew of the ship, with only one left to establish the duties of the master and the crew toward the PSCO, who should be treated with "courtesy and respect;"[48] the remaining 11 articles contemplate the duties of the PSCO toward the port State and the PSC system (refuse bribes, etc.).

To sum it up, the official statistics on the functioning of the various PSC regional systems, compared with the statistics on major maritime accidents, and together with some features of the legal instruments regulating PSC, suggest that port States are overly cautious in the exercise of their jurisdiction over foreign ships. This reluctance can be attributed to maritime and port traditions and comity—which, as seen in previous Chapters, are mirrored in the international and, to a lesser extent, European regulation of seaports—, but also to commercial expediency. After all, ships are the costumers of a port: without them, the port will not survive, and there is a fierce competition between seaports to attract sea lanes and shipping companies. This is implicitly recognized in the aforementioned Paris MoU Code of Conduct, insofar as it recommends to PSCOs not to base their decisions "on any commercial considerations of the port."[49]

Finally, further doubts on the effectiveness of Port State Control are raised by the Probo Koala case, which took place in 2006, well after the conclusion and the implementation of the Paris MoU. Between July 2 and 5, 2006, the Probo Koala, an oil tanker flying the Panama flag, called at the port of Amsterdam. A port worker rightly suspected the presence of toxic waste—specifically the so-called "slops," id est waste deriving from the cleaning of the tanks using acid substances—, and called in the port Authorities. The latter offered to dutifully dispose of the slops, at a cost of about 250,000 US dollars. From its HQ in London, the Dutch shipping company which had chartered the ship refused the offer. The Probo Koala was simply allowed the leave with its toxic waste, even if it was clear that the shipping company was not going to pay for a proper disposal of the waste, and could even unload it into the sea.

Afterwards, the ship called in the ports of Paldiski, Estonia (9–13 July) and Lagos, Nigeria (July 30–August 17), finally arriving to Abdjan, Ivory Coast, on 19

[44] Annex 1, paragraph 2.

[45] Annex 1, paragraph 3.

[46] Annex 1, paragraph 5.

[47] Annex 1, paragraph 10.

[48] Annex 1, paragraph 8.

[49] Annex 1, paragraph 24.

August.[50] There, the slopes were dumped in the slums outside Abdjan. A joint report issued by Greenpeace and Amnesty International after a three-year investigation, lists 43,492 confirmed cases and 24,825 likely cases of poisoning as a consequence of the dumping.[51]

The Probo Koala accident was the subject of judicial proceedings in the United Kingdom, the Netherlands, France, and the Ivory Coast.[52] Even the UN Human Rights Council adopted a report.[53] On July 23, 2010, the Amsterdam District Court, at the end of a criminal trial, imposed sentences to the ship commander,[54] an employee of the shipping company[55] and the shipping company itself.[56] The conviction of the shipping company was then partially quashed in appeal,[57] but, above all, the Amsterdam Port Authority and the local waste disposal company which, after an examination of the waste, pumped it back into the ship, were acquitted. The Port Authority, which, according to Dutch law, was the Municipality of Amsterdam, was acquitted for being a public entity acting in the exercise of public powers, and thus immune from criminal prosecution[58]; the disposal company successfully argued that it had followed the legitimate instructions of the Port Authority.[59] Both acquittals were upheld by the Supreme Court of the Netherlands.

The Probo Koala case has probably been the most important test case of Port State Control. Moreover, it involved an oil tanker, the very kind of ship which is supposed to be the main target of PSC. Unfortunately, not only the port of Amsterdam—one of the most advanced in the world, and one covered by the Paris MoU—failed the test, but the position adopted by the Netherlands judiciary on the case does not encourage hope in a greater assumption of responsibility by port authorities. This is obviously worrisome, especially taking into account the responsibility of port authorities in the War on Terror.

## References

Abuja MoU. (2012). Memorandum of Understanding Text. *Memorandum of understanding on port state control for west & central African region*. Retrieved from http://www.abujamou.org/index.php?pid=5t77uyggfgdf6756

---

[50]Fraser (2010).

[51]Amnesty International and Greenpeace Netherlands (2012), p. 54.

[52]Business & Human Rights Resource Centre (2016).

[53]United Nations (2009).

[54]District Court of Amsterdam (2010a).

[55]District Court of Amsterdam (2010b).

[56]District Court of Amsterdam (2010c).

[57]Amsterdam Court of Appeals (2011).

[58]District Court of Amsterdam (2010d).

[59]District Court of Amsterdam (2010e).

Allianz Global Corporate and Specialty SE. (2016). *Safety and shipping review 2016*, March 2016.
Amnesty International and Greenpeace Netherlands. (2012). *The toxic truth*. London-Amsterdam: Amnesty International Publications-Greenpeace Netherlands.
Amsterdam Court of Appeals. (2011). Judgment of 23 December 2011, case number 23-003334-10.
Argentine Naval Prefecture. (2012). *Acuerdo Latinoamericano sobre Control de Busques por el Estado Rector del Puerto*. Buenos Aires: Prefectura Naval Argentina.
Bang, H.-S. (2008). Is port state control an effective means to combat vessel-source pollution? *The International Journal of Marine and Coastal Law*, 23(4), pp. 715ff.
BBC. (2002). Striken oil tank sinks. *BBC*, November 19, 2002.
BBC. (2014). Why so many shipowners find Panama's flag convenient. *BBC*, August 5, 2014.
Black Sea MOU. (2016). BS MOU Text. *Black Sea MOU*. Retrieved from http://www.bsmou.org/
Brandon, M. (1953). Analysis of the terms "Treaty" and "International Agreement" for purposes of registration under article 102 of the United Nations charter. *The American Journal of International Law*, 47(1), pp. 52ff.
Business and Human Rights Resource Centre. (2016). Trafigura lawsuits (re Côte d'Ivoire). *Business and Human Rights Resource Centre*. Retrieved from https://business-humanrights.org/en/trafigura-lawsuits-re-c%C3%B4te-d%E2%80%99ivoire
Churchill, R. R., & Lowe, A. (1993). *The Law of the Sea*, II Rev. Ed. Manchester: Manchester University Press.
Chrisafis, A. (2008). The polluter pays: 30,000 tonne oil disaster costs French firm €200 m. *The Guardian*, January 17, 2008.
CMOU. (2010). About Us. *CMOU*. Retrieved from http://www.caribbeanmou.org/aboutus.php
District Court of Amsterdam. (2010a). Judgment of 23 July 2010, case number 13/846004-08 (PROMIS).
District Court of Amsterdam (2010b), Judgment of 23 July 2010, case number 13/864003-08 (PROMIS).
District Court of Amsterdam. (2010c). Judgment of 23 July 2010, case number 13/864003-06 (PROMIS).
District Court of Amsterdam. (2010d). Judgment of 23 July 2010, case number 13/846008-08.
District Court of Amsterdam. (2010e). Judgment of 23 July 2010, case number 13/846006-08 (PROMIS).
Dotinga, H., & Kwiatkowska, B. (Eds.). (2001). *International organizations and the law of the sea* (Vol. I). The Hague-London-Boston: Martinus Nijhoof Publishers.
Dunlap, W. W. (1996). Transit Passage in the Russian Arctic Straits. *Maritime Briefing*, 1996, 1 (7), pp. 1ff.
Elias, T. O. (1974). *The modern law of treaties*. Dobbs Ferry-Leiden: Sijthoff-Oceana.
Euronews. (2012). Erika, the globalised tanker disaster. *Euronews*, 25 September 2012.
FAO. (2002). *Implementation of the international plan of action to deter, prevent and eliminate illegal, unreported and unregolated fishing*. Rome: FAO.
Fraser, P. (2010). *The probo koala inquiry*. Singapore: Trafigura Group Pte. Ltd.
Hong Kong Special Administrative Region. (2016). *2015 Port of Hong Kong Statistical Tables*. Hong Kong: The Government of the Hong Kong Special Administrative Region of the People's Republic of China.
Indian Ocean Memorandum of Understanding on Port State Control. (2014). *Memorandum of Understanding on Port State Control for the Indian Ocean Region*, MOU.Rev 8 Oct 2014.
International Chamber of Shipping. (2016). *Shipping industry flag state performance table, 2015/2016*. London: International Chamber of Shipping.
International Maritime Organization (1991). *Regional cooperation in the control of ships and discharges*, Resolution A.682(17), adopted on November 6, 1991 (Agenda Item 10).
International Maritime Organization. (2016). Surveys, verifications and certification. *IMO*. Retrieved from http://www.imo.org/en/OurWork/MSAS/Pages/SurveysAndCertification.aspx
International Transport Workers' Federation. (2016). Defining FOCs and the problems they pose. *ITF Seafarers*. Retrieved from http://www.itfseafarers.org/defining-focs.cfm

Kasoulides, G. (1993). *Port state control and jurisdiction*. Netherlands: Springer.
LISCR. (2016). About the liberian registry. *Liberian Registry*. Retrieved from http://www.liscr.com/liscr/AboutUs/AboutLiberianRegistry/tabid/206/Default.aspx
McNair, A. D. (1961). *The law of treaties*. Oxford: Clarendon.
Mediterranean MoU. (2014). MoU Text. *Mediterranean M.O.U.* Retrieved from http://www.medmou.org/
Molenaar, E. J. (1998). *Coastal state jurisdiction over vessel-source pollution*. The Hague-Boston-London: Kluwer Law International.
Ozcayir, O. (2004). *Port state control, II Edition*. London-Singapore: Informa Professionals.
Panama Maritime Authority. (2015). About us. *The Panama Registry*. Retrieved from http://www.segumar.com/about-us/
Paris MoU (2016a). Memorandum. *Paris MoU*. Retrieved form https://www.parismou.org/about-us/memorandum
Paris MoU. (2016b). *Code of good practice for port state control officers conducting inspections within the framework of the Paris memorandum of understanding on port state control*, MSC/MEPC.4/circ. 2.
Port of Rotterdam. (2016). *An increase in the number of vessels in Rotterdam for the first time since 2007*, press release of February 26, 2016.
Quadri, R. (1939). *Le navi private nel diritto internazionale*. Milan: Giuffrè.
RINA Services s.p.a. (2016). RINA Services: About us. *RINA Services*. Retrieved from http://www.rina.org/en/aboutus
Riyadh MoU on PSC. (2015). Riyadh MoU text. *Riyadh memorandum of understanding*. Retrieved from http://www.riyadhmou.org/aboutmoutext.html
Rosenne, S. (1970). *The law of treaties*. Dobbs Ferry-Leiden: Sijthoff-Oceana.
Sands, P. (2012). *Principles of international environmental law* (III ed.). Cambridge: Cambridge University Press.
The International Tankers Owners Pollution Federation Limited. (2014). Amoco Cadiz, France, 1978. *ITOPF*. Retrieved from http://www.itopf.com/in-action/case-studies/case-study/amoco-cadiz-france-1978/
Tokyo MOU. (2016). Memorandum of Understanding. *Tokyo MOU*. Retrieved from http://www.tokyo-mou.org/organization/memorandum_of_understanding.php
Treves, T. (1995). *Il diritto del mare e l'Italia*. Milan: Giuffrè.
United Nations. (2009). *Report of the special rapporteur on the adverse effects of the movement and dumping of toxic and dangerous products and wastes on the enjoyment of human rights, Okechukwu Ibeanu*, A/HRC/12/26/Add.2.
United States Coast Guard. (2016). Foreign & Offshore Compliance Division (CG-CVC-2). *United States coast guard*. Retrieved from http://www.uscg.mil/hq/cgcvc/cvc2/psc/
Zwinge, T. (2011). Duties of flag states to implement and enforce international standards and regulations. *Journal of International Business and Law*, 10(2), pp. 297ff. Hempstead: Hofstra University.

# Chapter 15
# Port Security: The Dubai Ports World Case and the ISPS Code

The relationship between the War on Terror and seaports is little known to the public; and yet, a few facts will suffice to show it very clearly. A standard container has a 26,7 tons payload, and can be loaded with any kind of cargo,[1] including illegal cargo such as weapons, explosives or chemicals. Besides terrorist organizations, container can be used—and are used—also by common criminal organization to smuggle drugs, counterfeited goods, etc.

At the closure of the 2011 Fiscal Years on September 30, 2011—ten years after the Twin Towers attacks and the subsequent launch of the Container Security Initiative by the United States[2]—the U.S. Customs and Border Protection admitted that it was still able to inspect less than 5% of the containers handled in U.S. ports.[3]

In order to inspect a container, you have to open it, thus breaking the multimodal chain and delaying port operations. In theory, an alternative could be X-raying all the containers. However, due to their size, this has proven almost as unpractical as physical inspection.

The 5% figure is even more significant, in light of the fact that the official objective of the U.S. security policy would be a 100% inspection rate. The United States has planned to achieve this objective, not only using the X-ray technology, but pressing foreign ports into doing the same and hosting U.S. security officials, on a reciprocity basis.[4] However, so far the strategic economic role of seaports has caused container security to progress slowly at best.

Containers are not even mentioned in the 2002 International Ship and Port Facility Security (ISPS) Code,[5] a major diplomatic victory scored by the United States in the wake of the September 11 attacks.

---

[1]Gesamtverband der Deutschen Versicherungswirtschaft e.V. (2016).
[2]U.S. Department of Homeland Security (2016).
[3]Bliss (2012).
[4]Maritime Information Systems Ltd. (2016).
[5]International Maritime Organization (2002).

 
M. Casagrande, *Seaports in International Law*, SpringerBriefs in Law,
DOI 10.1007/978-3-319-60396-4_15

The Code was adopted as an amendment to the 1974 SOLAS Convention,[6] thus legally binding the States being Parties to the said Convention, which has reached a nearly universal adhesion.[7]

On a theoretical level, the Preamble of the Code is very significant, and specifically its point 5, in which the following two sentences can be found: "The extension of SOLAS 74 to cover port facilities was agreed on the basis that SOLAS 74 offered the speediest means of ensuring the necessary security measures entered into force and given effect quickly. However, it was further agreed that the provisions relating to port facilities should relate solely to the ship/port interface."

Once again, the law of the sea appears reluctant to enter the port domain, and when doing so, it maintains a strictly ancillary approach, treating the port only as a ship interface. At the same time, when the United States, after the September 11 attacks—which are expressly mentioned in the Preamble[8]—, felt the need to quickly innovate the international law applying to seaports, the only legal instrument available was a law of the sea treaty.

When it comes to the specific provisions of the Code applying to seaports, one would expect to find detailed rules on port security. For example, the 1979 ILO Dock Work Convention[9] lays down provisions on fencing,[10] lighting,[11] passageways,[12] etc. By contrast, in the ISPS Code the security measures to be taken by the port State are left to a Port Facility Security Plan,[13] to be adopted by the State itself. More precise technical norms—often rather vague anyway—can be found only in Part B of the Code. However, such norms, despite being included in the Code, are qualified as soft law rules or guidelines.[14]

In sum, the port specificity rule is strictly respected. As it is often the case for such rule, its application is partly justified, since every seaport has indeed its own peculiar features. However, it appears inappropriate to leave a matter such as security to the port clusters, which do not have the tools to fully handle it and, moreover, could see it only as a burden to the economy activity of the port.[15] The Code, in line with the general principles of international law, does not identify which State organs should draft, adopt and implement the PFSP, or which Government level should be competent in the matter. However, it appears to

---

[6]United Nations (1980).

[7]International Maritime Organization (2012).

[8]Point 2.

[9]International Labour Organization (1979).

[10]Article 8.

[11]Article 9.

[12]Article 10.

[13]Article 16.

[14]Preamble, point 9: "The guidance given in part B of this Code should be taken into account when implementing the security provisions set out in Chapter XI-2 of SOLAS 74 and in part A of this Code. However, it is recognized that the extent to which the guidance applies may vary depending on the nature of the port facility and of the ship, its trade and/or cargo."

[15]See Chap. 14.

assume that port security would be left to port clusters, in allowing State Parties to delegate part of their security duties to Recognized Security Organizations,[16] which appear as a revised version of the traditional Recognized Organizations/survey and certification companies, and whose required competences are as maritime as focused on security.[17]

If, on the one hand, port security should not be left entirely to port authorities and operators, on the other hand, it has few chances of working, if it is not taken seriously by port authorities.

The best indicator of the commitment of port authorities to port security would be the amount of money allocated to the latter. Unfortunately, the degree of financial transparency of port authorities is quite low, despite the fact that they are usually public bodies, or public-owned entities. Budget and financial reports are not made public, or are available only on a formal request, or in an extremely summary form.

No financial information at all was found on the Asian seaports. A check on the ten most important European seaports[18] was similarly fruitless. A check on the ten busiest U.S. seaports,[19] finally, allowed retrieving some information on the port authorities of Corpus Christi, Long Beach, Los Angeles, New York, and New Jersey.

The 2016 budget of the Port of Corpus Christi Authority provides only for "Safety/Environmental Expenses" and "Police Expenses." The latter, both direct and indirect, amount to 31,684 U.S. dollars and the total expenditures being 58,914,525 U.S. dollars.[20]

For the same fiscal year, the City of Long Beach Harbor Department plans to invest into security 26,388,775 U.S. dollars, the total budget being 829,130,000 U.S. dollars.[21]

In the fiscal year 2015/2016, the City of Los Angeles Harbor Department plans to invest in security 0.7% of its Capital Improvement Program of 198.8 million U.S. dollars.[22]

Finally, the Port Authority of New York and New Jersey earmarked for security 22% of its 2015 operating expenses and 2% of its 2015 capital expenditures.[23] The figure of operating expenses could suggest that the NY&NJ Port Authority—unsurprisingly, given its connection with the 2001 attacks—is particularly attentive to port security. However, it should be noted that this is a unique Port Authority, the

[16]Paragraph 4.3ff, Part B of the Code.

[17]Paragraph 4.5, Part B of the Code.

[18]Rotterdam, Antwerp, Hamburg, Amsterdam, Algeciras, Marseille, Le Havre, Immingham, Izmit and Botas. Source: Statistical Office of the European Union (2016).

[19]South Louisiana, Houston, New York, Beaumont, Long Beach, New Orleans, Corpus Christi, Baton Rouge, Los Angeles and Plaquemines. Source: U.S. Department of Transportation (2016).

[20]Port of Corpus Christi Authority (2015), pp. 1, 2.

[21]City of Long Beach Harbor Department (2015), pp. 2, 23.

[22]City of Los Angeles Harbor Department (2015), p. 8.

[23]The Port Authority of New York and New Jersey (2014), pp. 9, 10.

tasks of which go far beyond the management of the New York port. Founded in 1921 as an interstate agency, the Port Authority of New York and New Jersey has responsibility for five airports, including the John F. Kennedy International Airport and the LaGuardia Airport, four bridges, two tunnels connecting Manhattan, two bus terminals, a rail and subway system, a ferry system, two industrial areas, and three waterfronts.[24] It has its own Police Department, complete with air, firefighting, and special units.[25] Even so, considering the sum of operating and capital expenditures, the security budget is only 10.92% of the total, and no more than half of its percentage is likely to be allocated to port security.

Another key player of port security is terminal operators, to which the issue of port security probably reminds the US-DP World case. As said above,[26] DP World is a major international port operator; incorporated in the United Arab Emirates, it is largely State-owned.[27] In 2006, DP World acquired P&O, a major British port operator,[28] which managed some terminals in the U.S. ports of Baltimore, Miami, New Orleans, New York, and Philadelphia.[29] The possibility of a UAE State-owned port operator tasked with managing some of the most important U.S. terminals was almost immediately rejected by the U.S. Congress, which threatened to pass specific legislation in order to stop the takeover.[30] Yet, DP World had duly obtained clearance from the Committee on Foreign Investments in the United States.[31] Moreover, the White House itself came to the defense of DP World and the United Arab Emirates, which it considered a trusted ally in the War on Terrorism.[32] In particular, the White House noted that "UAE ports host more U.S. Navy ships than any port outside the United States. The UAE provides outstanding support for the U.S. Navy at the ports of Jebel Ali—which is managed by DP World—and Fujairah" (see Footnote 32). The Administration also pointed out that port security is not in the hands of terminal and ports operators[33] (although they are

[24]The Port Authority of New York and New Jersey (2016a).

[25]The Port Authority of New York and New Jersey (2016b).

[26]Chapter 12.

[27]Rotenberg (2007), p. 2.

[28]DP World (2016).

[29]Rotenberg (2007), p. 2.

[30]Rotenberg (2007), p. 2ff.

[31]Rotenberg (2007), p. 2. The Committee "is an inter-agency committee authorized to review transactions that could result in control of a U.S. business by a foreign person ('covered transactions'), in order to determine the effect of such transactions on the national security of the United States. CFIUS operates pursuant to Section 721 of the Defense Production Act of 1950, as amended by the Foreign Investment and National Security Act of 2007 (FINSA) (Section 721) and as implemented by Executive Order 11858, as amended, and regulations at 31 C.F.R. Part 800" (U.S. Department of the Treasury 2016). The FINSA Act was passed by the Congress in reaction to the DP World case (Folsom 2016, p. 288).

[32]Rotenberg (2007), p. 3.

[33]Rotenberg (2007), p. 6.

key players in ensuring it properly). In the end, DP World, under pressure by the U.S. Congress and public, transferred its U.S. operation.

It is impossible to say whether the DP World case curbed the enthusiasm of the U.S. Government for port security, or affected the will of the maritime-port community to cooperate in port security. Local port clusters, which are very often hostile to foreign takeovers, unsurprisingly opposed the deal. The States of Maryland, New York and New Jersey, acting in their capacity as Port Authorities, challenged in Court the authority of the federal Government to interfere with local port governance; the dockers' organizations similarly boycotted the DP Port takeover.[34] In the long run, however, the factor really affecting port security will be the reaction by major multinational port operators. While the reaction by DP World was subdued, there can be no doubt that its exclusion from the United States market was in violation of the standards which are ordinarily desired by foreign investors.

In the end, however, the reasons behind the lack of progress of port security are economical, logistical and technical. For the time being, no practical and realistic procedure has been discovered to inspect higher percentages of containers without impairing port operations; and the said operations simply cannot be stopped, because they are the cornerstone of globalized economy.

## References

Beisecker, R. (2006). DP World and U.S. port security. NTI, March 1, 2006.

Bliss, J. (2012). U.S. backs off all-cargo scanning goal with inspections at 4%. *Bloomberg*, August 13, 2012.

City of Long Beach Harbor Department. (2015). *Adopted budget for fiscal year 2016*. Long Beach: Port of Long Beach.

City of Los Angeles Harbor Department. (2015). *Adopted annual budget*. San Pedro: The Port of Los Angeles.

Folsom, Ralph. (2016). *Foreign investment law in a Nutshell*. St Paul: West Academic.

Gesamtverband der Deutschen Versicherungswirtschaft e.V. (2016). Standard containers. *TIS*. Retrieved from: http://www.tis-gdv.de/tis_e/containe/arten/standard/standard.htm

International Labour Organization. (1979). C152—Occupational Safety and Health (Dock Work) Convention, 1979 (No. 152). *International Labour Organization*. Retrieved from http://www.ilo.org/dyn/normlex/en/f?p=NORMLEXPUB:12100:0::NO::P12100_ILO_CODE:C152

International Maritime Organization. (2002). *Consideration and Adoption of the International Ship and Port Facility Security (ISPS) Code*, SOLAS/CONF.5/34.

International Maritime Organization. (2012). International Convention for the Safety of Life at Sea, 1974, as amended (SOLAS 1974). *IMO Documentation*. Retrieved from https://imo.amsa.gov.au/public/parties/solas74.html

Maritime Information Systems Ltd. (2016). Container security initiative: Just the facts. *Port Technology*. Retrieved from https://www.porttechnology.org/technical_papers/container_security_initiative_just_the_facts/

Port of Corpus Christi Authority. (2015). *2016 Annual Budget*. Corpus Christi: Port of Corpus Christi Authority.

[34]Beisecker (2006).

Rotenberg, J. J. (2007). *The Dubai ports world sebacle and its aftermath*. Harvard Business School Case 707-014, September 2006.
Statistical Office of the European Union. (2016). File:Top 20 cargo ports in 2014. *Eurostat*. Retrieved from http://ec.europa.eu/eurostat/statistics-explained/index.php/File:Top_20_cargo_ports_in_2014_-_on_the_basis_of_gross_weight_of_goods_handled_(in_million_tonnes).png
The Port Authority of New York and New Jersey. (2014), *2015 Budget*. New York: The Port Authority of New York and New Jersey.
The Port Authority of New York and New Jersey. (2016a). Overview of facilities and services. *The port authority of New York & New Jersey*. Retrieved from http://www.panynj.gov/about/facilities-services.html
The Port Authority of New York and New Jersey. (2016b). PAPD Services. *The Port Authority of New York & New Jersey*. Retrieved from: http://www.panynj.gov/police/services.html
United Nations. (1980). International Convention for the Safety of Life at Sea. *United Nations Treaty Series,1184*, pp. 277ff.
U.S. Department of Homeland Security. (2016). CSI: Container Security Initiative. *U.S. Customs and Border Protection*. Retrieved from https://www.cbp.gov/border-security/ports-entry/cargo-security/csi/csi-brief
U.S. Department of the Treasury. (2016). The Committee on Foreign Investment in the United States (CFIUS). *U.S. Department of the Treasury*. Retrieved from https://www.treasury.gov/resource-center/international/Pages/Committee-on-Foreign-Investment-in-US.aspx
U.S. Department of Transportation. (2016). Table 1-57. *United States Department of Transportation*. Retrieved from http://www.rita.dot.gov/bts/sites/rita.dot.gov.bts/files/publications/national_transportation_statistics/html/table_01_57.html

# Chapter 16
# From the Traditional to the Multimodal Seaport: The Right to Access

It is generally recognized that no ship is entitled to enter a foreign port unless she is in distress.[1] However, even this last assertion is incorrect, or at least should be qualified.[2] The obligation to grant shelter to a ship in distress does not bind the port State, but rather the coastal State.[3] The correct term to be used is not "port of refuge," but "place of refuge."[4] It is not only a matter of States jealously defending their reserved domain on seaports. Actually, a busy contemporary port could not be the best place to assist a ship in distress, especially in the case of dangerous or environment threatening marine accidents. At the same time, there is no denying that coastal State will often be reluctant to give shelter to a ship in distress, such as an oil spilling tanker. Significantly, IMO did not recommend to the Member State to draw and publish a list of the places of refuge made available, but rather an "event-specific assessment."[5]

The Montego Bay Convention does not innovate the traditional, restrictive regulation of port access, not even for land-locked States.[6] Even EU law does not explicitly grant ships flying a Member State flag the right to enter other Member States ports, although this right can be considered implicit.[7] Similarly, a right to access appears to be implicitly and indirectly granted by Article V of the General Agreement on Tariffs and Trade (GATT),[8] limited to vessels in transit.[9]

The lack of legal recognition of a right to access, for once, is not due—entirely, at least—to the low incidence of international regulation over seaports. In part, the

[1]Dugard (1981), p. 902; Dunlap (1996), p. 12; Özçayir (2003), p. 486ff.
[2]Morrison (2012), p. 53ff.
[3]Ringbom (2015), p. 144ff.
[4]IMO (2004); European Commission (2015).
[5]IMO (2004), paragraphs 3.4ff. See Chircop and Lindén (editors) (2006), p. 123ff.
[6]See Chap. 11.
[7]The right is made almost explicit by Article 1, paragraph 1 of Council Regulation (EEC) No 3577/92 (EU Council 1992), limited to maritime cabotage.
[8]World Trade Organization (1986).
[9]GATT, Article V, paragraph 1.

 
M. Casagrande, *Seaports in International Law*, SpringerBriefs in Law,
DOI 10.1007/978-3-319-60396-4_16

right to access issue is also of scarce practical relevance, since ships are routinely granted access to any foreign port without any difficulty, unless, of course, technical reasons prevent it. This is due, in part, to reasons of maritime comity, but, above all, to the fact that almost every contemporary port finances itself with the port dues and fees paid by ships. All over the world, port authorities will fight in order to attract more and more ships and traffic, and will not be willing to reject their primary users and costumers.

Any attempt to keep foreign operators outside the port market will thus focus on port services, which absorb the revenues generated by the ships rather than generating them: in fact, as seen above, in Europe such services are the front of a struggle for liberalization fought by the European Commission against local port operators and sympathetic European Institutions.[10]

In order to surpass the entry barriers to the port services market, in the framework of EU law, as seen above,[11] the treaty norms on the abuse of dominant position have been the main tool so far, since the attempt to adopt secondary legislation were less successful.

At least in one instance, however, the Commission applied to a seaport the so-called "essential facilities doctrine." Originated in the United States,[12] the essential facilities doctrine postulates that a subject in possession of a facility or infrastructure, which is essential to entry a relevant market, can be compelled to grant the use of such facility to a competitor, under reasonable conditions. The doctrine has found some degree of recognition in WTO law and other legal orders.[13]

After the famous 2004 Commission Decision in the Microsoft case,[14] EU law is often considered the new stronghold of the essential facilities doctrine, especially as the latter's role in U.S. law was greatly weakened by the nearly contemporary Trinko case.[15]

In a 1994 Decision,[16] the Commission declared that "the refusal of the Danish Government to allow 'Euro-Port A/S', a subsidiary of the Swedish group 'Stena Rederi AB' (Stena) to build a new port in the immediate vicinity of the port of Roedby (letter of 9 May 1990) or to operate from the existing port facilities at Roedby (letter of 8 August 1990) is incompatible with Article 90(1) of the EC Treaty, read in conjunction with Article 86."[17] Denmark was thus ordered to "bring to an end the infringement,"[18] and Stena was allowed to compete with a German

[10]See Chap. 13.

[11]Chap. 13.

[12]Supreme Court of the United States (1912).

[13]For a comparative approach, see Bavasso (2001); OECD (1996).

[14]European Commission (2004).

[15]Supreme Court of the United States (2004).

[16]European Commission (1994).

[17]European Commission (1994), Article 1.

[18]European Commission (1994), Article 2.

and Danish public undertaking in the market of ferry services for passengers and vehicles on the Roedby–Puttgarden route.[19]

The Roedby case, however, remains isolated, and, more generally, the essential facilities doctrine appears as the weakest legal tool in the Commission arsenal to use in the battle for port liberalization. Most U.S. legal scholar, indeed, concede that the doctrine is rather vague in its requirements, effects and limits.[20]

The European reenactment of the doctrine appears affected by the very same problems, at least in light of the Microsoft Decision. The said instrument, indeed, after a careful recognition of the European jurisprudence,[21] draws an exceedingly vague conclusion: "The case-law of the European Courts therefore suggests that the Commission must analyse the entirety of the circumstances surrounding a specific instance of a refusal to supply and must take its decision based on the results of such a comprehensive examination."[22] It is hardly surprising, therefore, then even EU law scholars, who usually have a more open and positive approach to the essential facilities doctrine, concede that it can and should be applied only in exceptional cases.[23]

It is therefore unlikely that the Commission will try to apply the essential facilities doctrine to ports, for various reasons. The doctrine vulnerable to criticism would be very difficult to apply to incredibly diverse and specialized ports and port services, and finally—due to its uncertainness—could not be appreciated by the main allies of the Commission in its struggle for port liberalization. These are the multinational port operators,[24] which, at least in Europe, are still in the process of overcoming the resistance by the traditional, local port operators.[25] Such multinational operators are themselves in a position of monopoly or oligopoly in many

---

[19]European Commission (1994), para 7.

[20]Maurer and Scotchmer (2013), p. 3: "These reactions are understandable. First, it is an antitrust doctrine that demands cooperation among rivals. This seems at odds with Section 1 of the Sherman Act, in which many forms of 'cooperation' are condemned. Instead of being suspicious of cooperation, the essential facilities doctrine demands it. How can these two bodies of law coexist? Second, many of the cases are brought and decided under Section 2 as refusal-to-deal cases, which has led scholars to ask whether an additional doctrine is necessary. Third, the doctrine's core cases span a bewildering array of facts and legal contexts. Some involve cooperative associations that span hundreds of parties; others just two. Some talk narrowly of feasible relief; others of a duty to share. It is tempting to avoid this chaos by getting rid of the doctrine entirely." Pitofski et al. (2002), p. 443: "Right of access to an essential facility controlled by a monopolist has long been a controversial subject under U.S. antitrust law... If U.S. scholarship were the last word on the subject, one would be led to conclude that the essential facilities doctrine should be described narrowly or fully abandoned."

[21]Paragraph 546ff.

[22]Paragraph 558.

[23]Massadeh (2011), p. 4; Turney (2005). Obviously, "a further difficulty of the 'exceptional circumstances'... is the definition of what is essential [in order to fulfill the exceptionality test]" (Turney 2005, p. 189).

[24]See Chap. 12.

[25]See Chap. 13.

maritime and port markets; moreover, in the long run, they can reasonably expect to overcome the resistance in some European ports and take control of their operation and services. In both scenarios, the essential facilities doctrine could play against them.

In light of these consideration, it is hardly surprising that the essential facilities doctrines is not referred in any way in the third Port Package adopted by the Commission,[26] the most recent attempt to reform and liberalize European ports.

Notwithstanding its practical relevance, the doctrine could play a role in an eventual systematic reshaping of international port law anyway. As it will be seen further on,[27] the construction of a scientifically autonomous international port law should start from a unitary notion of port. Such notion should undoubtedly take into account the multimodal nature of the contemporary port. In this respect, the essential facilities doctrine, since it is not limited to the traditional port facilities, could offer a legal argument to consider seaports in the framework of the multimodal chain, at least insofar as this is necessary to give a proper consideration to the land component of seaports.

## References

Bavasso, A. F. (2001). Essential facilities in EC law: The rise of an 'epithet' and the consolidation of a doctrine in the communications sector. *Yearbook of European Law, 21*(1), 63ff.

Chircop, A. E., & Lindén, O. (Eds.). (2006). *Places of refuge for ships*. Leiden-Boston: Martinus Nijhoff Publishers.

Council of the European Union. (2014). *Proposal for a regulation of the european parliament and of the council establishing a framework on market access to port services and financial transparency of ports (first reading)*. Interinstitutional File: 2013/0157 (COD).

Dugard, J. (1981). Jurisdiction over persons on board an aircraft landing in distress. *International and Comparative Law Quarterly, 30*(4), 902.

Dunlap, W. W. (1996). Transit passage in the arctic straits. *Maritime Briefing, 1*(7), 10.

EU Council. (1992). Council regulation (EEC) no 3577/92 of 7 December 1992 applying the principle of freedom to provide services to maritime transport within Member States (maritime cabotage). *Official Journal of the European Communities*, L 364, p. 7ff.

European Commission. (1994). Commission decision of 21 December 1993 concerning a refusal to grant access to the facilities of the port of Rødby (Denmark). *Official Journal of the European Communities*, L 055, p. 52ff.

European Commission. (2004). *Commission decision of 24.03.2004 relating to a proceeding under Article 82 of the EC Treaty (Case COMP/C-3/37.792 Microsoft)*. C(2004)900 final.

European Commission. (2015). *VTMIS places of refuge—EU operational guidelines*. Version 3-Final, 13 November 2015.

IMO. (2004). *Guidelines on places of refuge for ships in need of assistance*. Resolution A.949(23), Adopted on 5 December 2003 (agenda item 17), A 23/Res.949.

Massadeh, A. A. (2011). *The essential facilities doctrine under scrutiny: EU and US perspective*. UEA law school working paper series, UEA LAW WPS 2011-AM-1.

[26]EU Council (2014).

[27]Chap. 20.

Maurer, S. M., & Scotchmer, S. (2013). *The essential facilities doctrine: The lost message of terminal railroad*. Database of Berkeley—University of California. Retrieved from http://socrates.berkeley.edu/~scotch/EF.pdf

Morrison, A. P. (2012). *Places of refuge for ships in distress*. Leiden-Boston: Martinus Nijhoff Publishers.

OECD. (1996). *The essential facilities concept*. Paris: Organization for Economic Co-operation and Development.

Özçayir, Z. O. (2003). Ports of refuge. *The Journal of International Maritime Law, 9*, 486.

Pitofski, R., et al. (2002). The essential facilities doctrine under United States antitrust law. *Antitrust Law Journal, 70*(2002), 443.

Ringbom, H. (2015). *Jurisdiction over ships*. Leiden-Boston: Brill-Nijhoff.

Supreme Court of the United States. (1912). *United States v. Terminal Railroad Ass'n*. 224 U.S. 383.

Supreme Court of the United States. (2004). *Verizon Communications Inc. v. law offices of Curtis V. Trinko*. 540 U.S. 398.

Turney, J. (2005). Defining the limits of the EU essential facilities, doctrine on intellectual property rights: The primacy of securing optimal innovation. *Northwestern Journal of Technology and Intellectual Property, 3*(2), 179.

World Trade Organization. (1986). *The general agreement on tariffs and trade*. Geneva: World Trade Organization.

# Chapter 17
# Seaports in International Commercial Law

The usually pragmatic approach of international commercial law, on paper, would make this branch of international law a suitable tool to spearhead an international regulation of seaports.

Indeed, in the 1965 New York Convention on Transit Trade of Land-Locked States,[1] Article III applies the national treatment rule to ships flying the flag of land-locked States "as regards access to seaports and the use of such ports." The Convention appears to combine—and strengthen—some provision from the 1923 Geneva Convention on seaports[2] and from the contemporary Geneva Convention on railways,[3] which is the sign of a healthy multimodal approach. On the other hand, the UNCTAD Convention on International Multimodal Transport[4] failed to reach the required number of ratifications.[5]

Despite the UNCTAD Convention failure, in general international commercial law has the paradox of being even "too multimodal," id est of regulating the movement of goods in general, rather than their handling in a single segment of the transportation chain. This largely results from a concern to ensure the highest degree of legal certainty in the circulation of goods, avoiding that, in any controversy between buyer, seller, and carrier, the infinite and various accidents which can take place along the transport chain can be taken into consideration. Under this respect, a typical provision is Article 67(1) of the Vienna Convention on the International Sale of Goods[6]: "If the contract of sale involves carriage of the goods and the seller is not bound to hand them over at a particular place, the risk passes to the buyer when the goods are handed over to the first carrier for transmission to the buyer in accordance with the contract of sale..."

---

[1]United Nations (1967).
[2]See Chap. 7.
[3]League of Nations (1924).
[4]United Nations (1981).
[5]United Nations Conference on Trade and Development (2001), p. 18ff.
[6]United Nations (2010).



M. Casagrande, *Seaports in International Law*, SpringerBriefs in Law,
DOI 10.1007/978-3-319-60396-4_17

Another way in which international commercial law abstracts itself from the concrete functioning of the transport chain is its traditional reliance on shipping documents, such as the bill of lading.[7] Unsurprisingly, this long-standing—and undoubtedly efficient—document-based approach was maintained also in international commercial law instruments aiming at regulated the relationship between Member States and private operators, rather than between private operators, the main example being the TIR carnet, established by the TIR Convention[8] in order to facilitate the customs clearance of goods.[9]

This way, international commercial law "leapfrogs" the entire multimodal chain, which undoubtedly gives some benefits, but at the same times does not allow this branch of law to close the gap related to a specific legal study and regulation of seaports.

The same cannot be said of WTO law, in which it is possible to detect an attention for seaports, and in particular for the familiar topic of port liberalization.[10]

Within the WTO system, ports are seen under the lens of port services, covered by the General Agreement on Trade in Services.[11] In pursuing "progressive liberalization," the GATS provides for Member States to enter into successive rounds of negotiations,[12] during which the said States should, ideally, make commitments in order to achieve cross-border liberalization of services. Such commitments are set out in schedules,[13] which are available on the I-TIP Services database, managed jointly by the WTO and the World Bank.[14] In the database, port services are classified as "Services auxiliary to all modes of transport," under code 11.H. An interrogation to the database will show commitments by 59 Member States or assimilated subjects, such as the European Union and Hong Kong.[15] It is true that

[7]United Nations (1994); League of Nations (1932), as modified by United Nations (1985).

[8]United Nations (2013), p. 35.

[9]The parallel between the traditional bill of lading and the TIR carnet highlights the hybrid nature of international commercial law, stretching from public to private international law. Indeed, international commercial law is heavily studied and promoted by private international law bodies such as UNIDROIT (see UNIDROIT 2010), but—apart from the general consideration that private international law is often codified or promoted by international treaties—, some instruments, such as the TIR Convention, can hardly be classified as private international law. The relationship between public and private international law will emerge again in Chap. 19.

[10]See Chap. 13.

[11]World Trade Organization (2016a).

[12]Article XIX.

[13]Article XX.

[14]World Trade Organization (2016b).

[15]Albania, Armenia, Australia, Austria, Benin, Brazil, Bulgaria, Cabo Verde, Canada, China, Croatia, Cuba, Ecuador, Estonia, European Union, Finland, Georgia, Ghana, Hong Kong, Hungary, Iceland, Japan, Jordan, Kazakhstan, Kyrgyzstan, Latvia, Liberia, Liechtenstein, Lithuania, Macedonia, Malaysia, Mexico, Moldova, Montenegro, Nepal, New Zealand, Norway, Oman, Philippines, Russia, Saint Lucia, Saint Vincent and the Grenadines, Saudi Arabia, Seychelles, Sierra Leone, Singapore, Slovenia, South Korea, Switzerland, Taiwan, Tajikistan, Thailand, Tonga, Ukraine, United States of America, Uruguay, Venezuela, Viet Nam, and Yemen.

many of these States are not major port hubs, or are even land-locked States. However, the major port players are indeed present: the European Union Member States, Japan and, above all, China. The mere existence of commitments, however, is not per se a warranty of liberalization.

Using as sample the crucial subsector of cargo-handling services, the user will discover that:

(a) Armenia, Brazil, Cabo Verde, China, Croatia, Ecuador, Georgia, Hungary, Japan, Kazakhstan, Lithuania, Philippines, South Korea, Taiwan, Ukraine, Venezuela, and Viet Nam do not allow cross-border supply, id est the contentious cargo self-handling;
(b) Australia, Bulgaria, the European Union, Finland, Malaysia, Mexico, New Zealand, Saint Lucia, Saint Vincent and the Grenadines, Slovenia, Thailand, Tonga, and the United States have no commitments at all;
(c) Benin will allow only "container stuffing and destuffing";
(d) Cuba's commitments are limited to transhipment in Havana and Mariel, or at terminals specialized in the handling of fertilizers;
(e) Hong Kong, Montenegro, and Russia expressly exclude from its commitments the dockers organizations.

Overall, from the GATS schedules it is possible to draw a picture in which most ports are now open to worldwide terminal operators. In some States, they will be required to establish a local corporation, in some instances involving local shareholders; similar obstacles, however, are easy to overcome by multinational corporations, the practice of which will often provide for the establishment of national subsidiaries in their own right. Self-handling, however, remains a rare exception, and even the practice of open door to foreign terminal operators described above has very significant exceptions, such as the United States, the European Union, Hong Kong, and Russia. In the case of Hong Kong and Russia, the wording of the commitments clearly shows a continuing influence by port workers organizations; the same influence is surely operating in the European Union, as seen above.[16]

As the only major port player which did not make any commitment in the cargo handling subsector—since the United States only has relatively minor ports, the European Union indeed confirms itself as a veritable stronghold of the port workers organizations, at least for the time being.

The jurisprudence of the WTO quasi-judicial bodies, on the other hand, includes at least an interesting case, which is not—as one could suppose—the dispute between the EU and the United States on the US Harbour Maintenance Tax,[17] but a

[16]Chap. 13.

[17]The dispute was opened by a Request for Consultations presented by the European Union in 1998 (World Trade Organization 1998). However, the dispute has not had any follow up since then, and it is only loosely related to seaports anyhow. The Harbour Maintenance Tax, also known as Harbour Maintenance Fees, in fact, cannot be considered a port fee or due, since it is levied on the value of the cargo shipped through U.S. ports, without any correlation with the port services supplied to the ship or the logistical operator (U.S. Customs and Border Protection 2016).

2007 case involving Colombia, which, inter alia, "on 12 July 2005... introduced a measure requiring those subject textiles, appareland footwear originating in or arriving from Panama and China to enter only at Bogota airport or Barranquilla seaport."[18] Upholding the arguments put forward by Panama, a WTO panel, after considering the actual situation of logistics between the two countries, ruled that such as measures is a quantitative restriction, pursuant to Article XI of GATT,[19] thus establishing a link between the right to access to ports[20] and the free movement of goods.

However, the Colombian case is likely to remain isolated,[21] simply because the Colombian measure is unlikely to be adopted by another State. In fact, in a context of fierce competition between seaports, any measure to restrict imports—even in the framework of protectionist policies—would not take the form of a denial of access to seaports. Indeed, denying access to all seaports and not to airports, railways, and roads would be unnecessary violation of maritime comity; such a measure would make sense only if the interested State wanted to privilege commerce with States sharing a border with itself. Restricting access to only some ports would be similarly difficult, given the competition between national ports.

## References

American Association of Port Authorities. (2014). *'Hit the HMT target!' Letter amasses over 400 backers; Moves to congress*, October 22, 2014.

League of Nations. (1924). *Records and texts relating to the convention and statute of the international regime of railways* (p. 85ff). Geneva: League of Nations.

League of Nations. (1932). International convention for the unification of certain rules relating to bills of lading. In *League of Nations Treaty Series* (Vol. CXX, p. 157ff).

McIntosh, C. R., et al. (2015). Paying for harbor maintenance in the US: Options for moving past the harbor maintenance tax. *Transportation Research, 74,* 210ff.

(Footnote 17 continued)

Furthermore, the tax is not managed by Port Authorities, the revenues being appropriated by a Harbour Maintenance Trust Fund, which is managed directly by the U.S. Congress. The Fund is supposed to finance port maintenance, but this does not happen, because the Congress routinely does not authorize the use of the funds, or diverts them to different purposes (Washington Council on International Trade 2011; American Association of Port Authorities 2014; further flaws of the tax are highlighted by McIntosh et al. 2015).

[18]World Trade Organization (2007), par. 2.2.

[19]World Trade Organization (2007), par. 7.275.

[20]Chap. 16.

[21]It is worth noting that the European Union, intervening as a third party in the Colombia case, argued that a partial closure of seaports to foreign goods could not be considered a restriction. At most, it could be considered a violation of the most-favored-nation treatment principle, pursuant to Article I of GATT, insofar as it was applied only to Panama (World Trade Organization 2007, par. 5.33ff).

UNIDROIT. (2010). *Unidroit principles*. Rome: International Institute for the Unification of Private Law.

United Nations. (1967). Convention on transit trade of land-locked states. In *United Nations Treaty Series* (Vol. 8641, p. 4ff).

United Nations. (1981). *United Nations conference on a convention on international multimodal transport*. New York: United Nations.

United Nations. (1985). Protocol to amend the international convention for the unification of certain rules of law relating to bills of lading. In *United Nations Treaty Series* (Vol. 1412, p. 127ff).

United Nations. (1994). *United Nations convention on the carriage of goods by sea*. New York: United Nations.

United Nations. (2010). *United Nations convention on contracts for the international sale of goods*. New York: United Nations.

United Nations. (2013). *TIR handbook* (tenth revised ed.). New York and Geneva: United Nations.

United Nations Conference on Trade and Development. (2001). *Implementation of multimodal transport rules*. UNCTAD/SDTE/TLB/2.

U.S. Customs & Border Protection. (2016). *Harbor maintenance fees (HMF)*. U.S. Customs and Border Protection. Retrieved from https://help.cbp.gov/app/answers/detail/a_id/283/~/harbor-maintenance-fees-(hmf)

Washington Council on International Trade. (2011). *Reform the harbor maintenance tax*. Seattle: Washington Council on International Trade.

World Trade Organization. (1998). *United States—Harbour maintenance tax*. WT/DS118/1.

World Trade Organization. (2007). *Colombia—Indicative prices and restrictions on ports of entry*. WT/DS366/R.

World Trade Organization. (2016a). *General agreement on trade in services*. World Trade Organization. Retrieved from https://www.wto.org/english/docs_e/legal_e/26-gats_01_e.htm

World Trade Organization. (2016b). *I-TIP services*. I-TIP Services. Retrieved from http://i-tip.wto.org/services/default.aspx

# Part V
# Assessment and Perspectives

# Chapter 18
# Common Features in the International Regulation of Seaports

The previous chapters are an attempt to recompose the fragmented picture of international and European port regulation. In choosing the pieces to put together, I was consciously quite selective, looking for legal norms regulating specifically seaports, rather than norms incidentally applying to ports.

A typical example of this last kind of norms could be those establishing standards for ships. It is true that such rules are de facto enforced in seaports,[1] and sometimes even implemented there, as it is case for some standards on waste disposal, which require the establishment of specific facilities in seaports. However, my experience as a researcher focused on seaports, earned especially during my doctorate at Padua University, shows that such norms will have some sort of vis attractiva, which operates in two different ways. Firstly, they will bring with them a mass of other rules, legal doctrine and jurisprudence from their own field (law of the sea, shipping law, transportation law, etc.). Secondly, this mass, being much more voluminous and à la page than anything specifically regarding ports, will quickly draw the legal discourse away from such subject.

In the case of colonial factories,[2] specific norms simply could not be found; however, this could be due to the ancient origin of such ports and the unequal international relations which led to their establishment.

In other cases, the few norms mentioning seaports proved to be focused on other issues. Paolo Sarpi treated ports as maritime accessories,[3] and so did the international judges or State legal officers handling the Lotus case, the Kiel Canal case and the Suez crisis.[4] The very few articles of the Montego Bay Convention mentioning seaports consider them mainly for the purposes of territorial waters demarcation.[5] The essential facilities doctrine, which was applied by the European Commission to

[1]See Chap. 14.
[2]See Chap. 5.
[3]See Chap. 4.
[4]See Chap. 8.
[5]See Chap. 11.



M. Casagrande, *Seaports in International Law*, SpringerBriefs in Law,
DOI 10.1007/978-3-319-60396-4_18

the Danish port of Rodby,[6] is obviously not focused on ports, but on infrastructures in the amplest meaning of the term.

Even when the international community, the European Institutions, the legal scholars, or the international school appear finally ready to tackle the port issue,[7] inevitably something seems to go wrong. Attempts at creating an international or European regulation of seaports are unable to materialize as binding legal instruments.[8] If they do, such instruments are not applied or enforced[9]; and if they are, they remain isolated.[10]

It can hardly be said that this lack of attention for seaports can be attributed to a low practical relevance of the latter. As seen above, seaports have become critical junctions of globalization,[11] and even in the War on Terror.[12] However, the crucial importance of seaports was not established in the contemporary era. Well before that, seaports were symbols of Imperial power, such as the Venice Arsenal or the London Docks,[13] or globally strategical hotspots, such as the colonial factories or Tangiers.[14]

The legal tendency to overlook seaports was probably born out of theoretical reasons, arising from their borderline nature, between the law of the sea and other branches of international law. In an era in which international relations were based on strength, rather than international rules, such a formal approach was not particularly troublesome; the silence of legal scholars on a sensitive issue like seaports was perhaps even relished by Governments. Furthermore, early international law was heavily influenced by Roman law, which, in turn, did not have a particular focus on seaports, or even on maritime law.[15]

In the modern and contemporary age, more mundane factors added to this traditional theoretical framework. Between XIX and XX centuries, seaports often became fiefs of port workers organizations, which had every interest in maintaining seaports as self-contained environments, overemphasizing port specificity and even

---

[6]See Chap. 16.

[7]This often happens under the pressure of extreme circumstances, such as major international crises (see Chap. 9), strings of disastrous oil spills (see Chap. 14) or the September 11 attacks (see Chap. 15).

[8]The various attempts by the European Commission to reform the port sector (see Chap. 13); the negotiations on port services within WTO (see Chap. 17).

[9]The Mar del Plata Convention (see Chap. 10); the Port State Control MoUs (see Chap. 14); the ISPS Code (see Chap. 15).

[10]The few ILO Convention on port work (see Chap. 6); the 1923 Geneva Convention on seaports (see Chap. 7); the port rules in the laws of war (see Chap. 9); the port of Genoa case in EU law (see Chap. 13).

[11]Chap. 13.

[12]Chap. 15.

[13]Chap. 1.

[14]Chap. 5.

[15]See Digesta, Boox XIV, Title II, which merely incorporated the Rhodian jettison rules.

snubbing international labor rules.[16] Ironically, this is making easier for multinational port operators to take over the traditional port communities, which are made weaker by their partly self-imposed isolation.

Any attempt to change this trend, even when triggered by the most pressing constraints, has so far proved short-lived, a striking example being the ISPS Code, which was adopted after the September 11 attacks.[17] At first sight, the Code appears a huge diplomatic success and a rare, clear assumption of responsibilities by the international community: indeed, it was adopted in record time, and is binding for almost every State. However, at a closer look, it reveals itself as a manifesto for port specificity, ultimately leaving to every seaport the decision on how to ensure its own security.

A similar pattern can ben detected in the evolution of EU law and practice. After the cutting-edge decision in the port of Genoa case by the Court of Justice, the European Commission was stopped by the European Parliament and the Council in its attempt to implement the judgment and further promote its principles.[18]

In 2013, the Commission drafted a third Ports Package,[19] which, while containing an adequate and progressive definition of seaport,[20] cannot be considered a true reform or harmonization of EU ports.[21]

The overall picture of a weak international and EU legal framework is exacerbated by the circumstance that port law must face a heavier burden than most other branches of law: it has to overcome the resistance to legal regulation which is maintained—for very different reasons—by the old and new port actors. Such resistance not only prevents the production of specific, robust, and organic rules on seaports, as seen above, but, when such rules do exist, it is often able to silently hinder their implementation and enforcement.

A blatant example of this trend is port State jurisdiction, which, by its very nature, should be a cornerstone of port law. As seen above,[22] most scholars agree that the exercise of port State jurisdiction has never had any real obstacle in the international law in force. However, the said jurisdiction is not extensively

[16]Chap. 6.

[17]Chap. 15.

[18]Chap. 13.

[19]European Commission (2013a).

[20]Art. 2(16).

[21]Pursuant to Art. 6, the Port Authority (the "managing body of the port") can limit the number of service providers within the port, even citing a vague criterion such "public service obligations." It should be kept in mind that, according to the Commission itself, services of general economic interest (SGEIs) are "not defined in the TFEU or in secondary legislation," therefore "the concept may apply to different situations and terms, depending on the Member States, and EU law does not create any obligation to designate formally a task or a service as being of general economic interest" (European Commission 2013b, pp. 21–22). Furthermore, the proposed Regulation "shall not affect the application of the social and labour rules of the Member States" (Art. 10). Above all, most of the Regulation would not apply to "cargo handling services and passengers services" (Art. 11): the bulk of port activities.

[22]Chap. 14.

regulated in the Montego Bay Convention[23] and is generally recognized as contrary to international comity or practice.[24] Therefore, even when its exercise is made compulsory by Port State Control Memorandum of Understandings, the available data, as well as cases such as the Probo Koala one, consistently show that this does not happen in practice.[25]

Since the current legal and practical situation does not appear sustainable in a globalized world in which seaports are vital economic and security hubs, international and EU "lawmakers" (States, international organizations and EU Institutions) should address the port regulation issue with a clear show of political will, while remaining open to the legitimate needs of port communities and operators. The adoption of legal norms tailored on seaports, rather than incidentally regulating them, appears essential for this purpose. Legal scholars, by their part, should treat port law as a relevant, scientifically autonomous discipline.

## References

European Commission. (2013a). *Proposal for a Regulation Of The European Parliament And Of The Council establishing a framework on market access to port services and financial transparency of ports*, /* COM/2013/0296 final - 2013/0157 (COD)*/.

European Commission. (2013b). *Commission staff working document—Guide to the application of the European Union rules on state aid, public procurement and the internal market to services of general economic interest, and in particular to social services of general interest*. SWD (2013) 53 final/2.

Marten, Bevin. (2014). *Port state jurisdiction and the regulation of international merchant shipping*. Cham: Springer.

[23]Chap. 11.

[24]Chap. 8. In the most recent and complete appraisal of port State jurisdiciton, Marten (2014), while concluding, that, in purely legaly terms, the exercise of port State jurisdiction has always been allowed and is even being extended, admits that "states often refrain from exercising jurisdiction over many aspects of the merchant vessels visiting their ports" (p. 224). Significantly, such restraint is due to the resistance by economic operators, rather than by Governments (p. 228ff.).

[25]Ibidem.

# Chapter 19
# A Contribution from Private International Law and Some Municipal Legal Orders

Van Hooydonk, one of the few specialized port law scholars, admits that seaports are, for theoretical as well as practical reasons, "particularly recalcitrant subjects of legal regulation."[1] He adopts a dual attitude to the problem, partly downplaying it and partly attempting to tackle it with a multidisciplinary approach, which is, in turn, strong and multifaceted at the same time. Indeed, van Hooydonk considers port law as a branch of maritime law, without distinguishing between its international, European and internal provisions.[2]

The idea of an osmosis between international and municipal law (including private international law) is tempting, because internal law can appear as more progressive and less resistant to change than international law in the port field. On the one hand, many States have reformed or are in the process of reforming their port sector[3]; on the other hand, private international law has proven able, at less in some instances, to overcome firmly established principles and practices, such as the usual noninterference of port authorities in the affairs of foreign ships.[4]

However, even setting aside any issue related to its theoretical foundations, such an approach would be of dubious practical utility. The new municipal legislation on seaports appears focused on deregulation, rather than attempting to construct an organic framework of port law.

---

[1]Van Hooydonk (2010), p. 30.
[2]Van Hooydonk (2010), p. 34.
[3]For Argentina, see Presidencia de la Nación (1992). For Australian State legislation, see Ports Australia (2016). For Brazil, see Presidência da República (2016). For China, see Central People's Government of the People's Republic of China (2016). For Italy, see Istituto Poligrafico e Zecca dello Stato (2016). For New Zealand, see New Zealand Government (2016). For Nigeria, see Food and Agriculture Organization of the United States (2016). For Spain, see Agencia Estatal Boletín Oficial del Estado (2011). See also World Bank Group (2012).
[4]See Chap. 14; on the ability of international private law to deviate from this practice, see Carbone and Schiano di Pepe (2010), p. 155ff.



M. Casagrande, *Seaports in International Law*, SpringerBriefs in Law,
DOI 10.1007/978-3-319-60396-4_19

The US Cruise Vessel Security and Safety Act 2000[5] could be considered at least a partial exception. Indeed the Act, while being mainly concerned with ship standards and cruise company obligations, applies to ships which are "on a voyage that embarks or disembarks passengers in the United States,"[6] which is per se a very progressive provision. However, it should be kept in mind that the Act was enacted under exceptional circumstances, after the US Congress realized that flag State jurisdiction, besides its other shortcomings,[7] has been posing a real and substantial risk for the life and the security of passengers on cruise ships, due to the lack of jurisdiction of port and coastal authorities, and the inability of the unwillingness of flag State bodies (mainly the ship master) to investigate crimes.[8] The Act thus compels ships to abide to some security standards (such as surveillance systems) and to report crimes which took place onboard to US Authorities. Given the astounding data collected by the US Coast Guard in the enforcement of the Act,[9] it is only surprising that this US legislation has not been imitated by other States, or incorporated into an international instrument. The mere fact that the issue was addressed only in 2010, and only in the United States—a State with the bargaining power needed to disregard maritime comity and international practice, suggests instead that the Act will remain isolated.

As for private international law, its extension of port State jurisdiction was motivated mainly by the necessity of protecting seafarers.[10] Private international law has thus stayed in line with the traditional rules of maritime comity, but it is highly dubious that it would adopt a similar progressive stance, when doing so would contradict traditional tenets of maritime tradition, such as port specificity.

In the end, an attempt to overcome the well-established conceptual borders between legal orders, in order to start to build a coherent set of port law rules, could be tantamount to renouncing to sound theoretical foundations, without even achieving significant practical results. Indeed, the factors which have been hindering the development of port law operate at the international, EU, and municipal levels. It is therefore preferable to stick to traditional legal reasoning and work for the development of port law within the boundaries of international law.

[5]U.S. House of Representatives (2016); Title 46, Chap. 35.

[6]§3507(g)(1)(A)(iii).

[7]Chap. 14.

[8]Lloyd (2014).

[9]Between 1 July and 30 September 2016, cruise companies reported to the US Coast Guard 1 suspected death, 1 missing US national, 3 serious assaults and, above all, 16 sexual assaults (U.S. Department of Transportation 2016).

[10]Carballo Piñeiro (2016).

## References

Agencia Estatal Boletín Oficial del Estado. (2011). Texto Refundido de la Ley de Puertos del Estado y de la Marina Mercante. *Boletín Oficial del Estado*, October 20, 2011, n. 253, p. 109456.

Carballo Piñeiro, L. (2016). Port state jurisdiction over labour conditions: A private international law perspective on extra-territoriality. *The International Journal of Marine and Coastal Law, 31*(3), 531ff.

Carbone, S. M., & Schiano di Pepe, L. (2010). *Conflitti di sovranità e di leggi nei traffici marittimi tra diritto internazionale e diritto dell'Unione europea*. Turin: Giappichelli.

Food and Agriculture Organization of the United Nations. (2016). *Nigerian Ports Authority Act*. FAOLEX. Retrieved from http://faolex.fao.org/docs/pdf/nig61964.pdf

Istituto Poligrafico e Zecca dello Stato. (2016). Decreto legislativo 4 agosto 2016, n. 169. *Gazzetta Ufficiale della Repubblica Italiana*, n. 203 of August 31, 2016.

Lloyd, M. (2014). *The investigation of incidents and crime at sea*. Retrieved from http://cruisevictims.homestead.com/THE_INVESTIGATION_OF_ACCIDENTS_AND_CRIME_AT_SE1-final.pdf

New Zealand Government. (2016). *Port Companies Act 1988*. New Zealand Legislation. Retrieved from http://www.legislation.govt.nz/act/public/1988/0091/latest/DLM131683.html

People's Government of the People's Republic of China. (2016). *Port law of the People's Republic of China*. China.org.cn. Retrieved from http://www.china.org.cn/english/DAT/214825.htm

Ports Australia. (2016). *Links*. Ports Australia. Retrieved from http://www.portsaustralia.com.au/about/links#Legislation

Presidência da República. (2016). *Ley N° 12.815, de 5 de junho de 2013*. Planalto. Retrieved from http://www.planalto.gov.br/ccivil_03/_ato2011-2014/2013/Lei/L12815.htm

Presidencia de la Nación. (1992). Desregulacion de la actividad portuaria. *Boletín Oficial*, 26 June 1992.

U.S. Department of Transportation. (2016). *Cruise Vessel Security and Safety Act (CVSSA) statistical compilation*. Transportation.gov. Retrieved from https://www.transportation.gov/sites/dot.gov/files/docs/Cruise%20Line%20Incident%20Report%20-%201%20Jul%20-%2030%20Sep%202016.pdf

U.S. House of Representatives. (2016). *United States code*. Retrieved from http://uscode.house.gov/

Van Hooydonk, E. (2010). *The Law ends where the port ara begins*. Maklu: Antwerpen-Apeldoorn-Portland.

World Bank Group. (2012). *Port reform toolkit PPIAF* (2nd ed.). PPPIRC. Retrived from https://ppp.worldbank.org/public-private-partnership/library/port-reform-toolkit-ppiaf-world-bank-2nd-edition

# Chapter 20
# Starting from a Unitary Notion of Port

In order to achieve a scientifically autonomous, adequate international port law, the only way which is open is the classical one: work within the realm of international law as a separate legal order.

A starting point should be a unitary notion of port. That would be a neutral, technical, definitory approach which should not meet too much resistance from the academic world and, perhaps more importantly, port clusters.

Moreover, the framing of a definition of seaports is the task in which EU and municipal law—while remaining separate from international law—can offer the most valuable starting points.

The last Port Package proposed by the European Commission[1] states that "'seaport' means an area of land and water made up of such works and equipment so as to permit, principally, the reception of ships, their loading and unloading, the storage of goods, the receipt and delivery of these goods and the embarkation and disembarkation of passengers; and any other infrastructure necessary for transport operators within the port area."[2]

Similarly, according to the port law of China—by far the country were the most important ports are located[3], "the term 'port' means a region comprising certain water and land areas, having the functions for vessels to enter, leave, lie at anchor and moor, for passengers to embark and disembark, and for goods to be loaded, unloaded, lightered and stored, and being equipped with the necessary dock facilities."[4]

These are both progressive definitions of seaport, since they take into due consideration the land component of the port, as well as the water one.

---

[1]European Commission (2013).
[2]Art. 2(16). See also European Union (2005).
[3]See Chap. 12.
[4]Legislative Affairs Commission of the Standing Committee of the National People's Congress (2003), Article 3.



M. Casagrande, *Seaports in International Law*, SpringerBriefs in Law,
DOI 10.1007/978-3-319-60396-4_20

This balance cannot be taken for granted. For example, according to the US Code[5] "'seaport' means all piers, wharves, docks, and similar structures, adjacent to any waters subject to the jurisdiction of the United States, to which a vessel may be secured, including areas of land, water, or land and water under and in immediate proximity to such structures, buildings on or contiguous to such structures, and the equipment and materials on such structures or in such buildings."[6] Waters are thus deemed relevant only when "in immediate proximity" to terrestrial structures.

An UNCTAD report on municipal port law,[7] quoting Grosdidier de Matons and a Colombian statute, defines a seaport as "a place on the coast specially designated by the competent administrative authority to serve the purposes of seaborne trade" or "an area of land and water made up of such improvement works and equipment as to permit, principally, the reception of ships, their loading and unloading, the storage of goods, the receipt and delivery of these goods by inland transport and can also include the activities of businesses linked to sea transport."[8]

The land component of the port is thus generally dominant in municipal law. For example, in France seaports are expressly excluded from the jurisdiction of the Maritime Prefect.[9] On the other hand, in some States the Military or Merchant Navy has had a significant role in the administration of civilian seaports, usually through the Harbour Master's Office.[10] In the Hong Kong legislation, for example, a port is "any area of the waters of Hong Kong" so declared by the Secretary for Transport and Housing.[11]

The drafting of an international notion of seaport should therefore start from a progressive definition, such as those found in EU and Chinese law. In these legal orders, it is possible to find a correct balance of the land and sea component of seaports, as well as between service to ships (and passengers) and the handling of goods: in contemporary ports, containers are just as important as ships.

That means considering seaports as elements in the multimodal chain, rather than isolatedly. In the long run, an ideal outcome would be to adopt a "fading" or "concentric" notion of port, by which some port law rules (for example, technical standards, right to access rules, transport goodsents and inspection rules) apply not only within the port, but to the whole multimodal chain. According to the Italian port law,[12] for example, port authorities have a limited power to adopt urban planning rules.[13]

---

[5]U.S. House of Representatives (2016).

[6]Title 18, Ş. 26.

[7]UNCTAD Secretariat (1993).

[8]UNCTAD Secretariat (1993), p. 23.

[9]French Republic (2017), Art. 1.

[10]International Harbour Masters' Association (2017).

[11]The Government of the Hong Kong Special Administrative Region of the People's Republic of China (2017), Chapter 313, Section 56.

[12]State Printing Service and Mint (1994).

[13]Article 5.

Unfortunately, any serious consideration of port law at an international level would require a real commitment by legal scholars and a lack of opposition by port actors. Both these conditions are unlikely to realize. In academia, there are few signs of interests for seaports. Moreover, in the contemporary, highly sophisticated legal studies, the historic lack of specific studies on seaports, and thus of material and references, makes difficult to kick-start this new field, in some sort of "loop effect."

As for port actors, the traditional ones could become less resistant to legal regulation, having being weakened by globalization. On the other hand, multinational port operators have any interest in taking advantage of the existing legal limbo, or even pressing for more deregulation.

In the long run, much will depend on the process of globalization. One could be tempted to take for granted that our world is becoming more and more interconnected, thus making seaports vital hubs in clear need of some international regulation. However, as emerging countries start targeting their huge internal markets, rather than external ones, this trend could change, at least for the international movement of goods.

The international maritime industry is indeed already facing a significant crisis,[14] although it is too early to tell if it is due to sector-related causes or the 2009 crisis, or rather the signal of a deeper, global trend.

## References

European Commission. (2013). *Proposal for a regulation of the european parliament and of the council establishing a framework on market access to port services and financial transparency of ports*, /* COM/2013/0296 final - 2013/0157 (COD) */.

European Union. (2005). Directive 2005/65/EC of the European Parliament and of the Council of 26 October 2005 on enhancing port security. *Official Journal of the European Union* L 310 of 25 November 2005, p. 28.

Ficenec, J. (2016). Zombie ships send maritime freight into worst crisis in living memory. *The Telegraph*, January 22, 2016.

French Republic. (2017). *Décret n°2004-112 du 6 février 2004 relatif à l'organisation de l'action de l'Etat en mer*. Legifrance. Retrieved from https://www.legifrance.gouv.fr/affichTexte.do?cidTexte=JORFTEXT000000611843&fastPos=3&fastReqId=430002349&categorieLien=cid&oldAction=rechTexte

Hanjin Shipping Co., Ltd. (2012). *Overview*. Hanjin Shipping. Retrieved from http://www.hanjin.com/hanjin/CUP_HOM_1700.do?sessLocale=en

Informa UK Limited. (2016). *Hanjing Shipping*. Lloyd's list. Retrieved from https://onedrive.live.com/view.aspx?resid=F44B54F543003C2B!1777&app=Word

International Harbour Masters' Association. (2017). *Training and education*. IHMA. Retrieved from http://www.harbourmaster.org/hm-training-education.php

[14]Ficenec (2016), UNCTAD (2016), pp. 17–18. Particularly shocking was the 2016 bankruptcy of Korean company Hanjin Shipping (Informa UK Limited 2016), which used to be in first ten container carriers worldwide (Hanjin Shipping Co., Ltd. 2012).

Legislative Affairs Commission of the Standing Committee of the National People's Congress. (2003). *Port law of the People's Republic of China.* china.org.cn. Retrieved from http://www.china.org.cn/english/DAT/214825.htm

State Printing Service and Mint. (1994). Legge 28 gennaio 1994, n. 84. *Gazzetta Ufficiale della Repubblica Italiana*, n. 28 of February 4, 1994.

The Government of the Hong Kong Special Administrative Region of the People's Republic of China. (2017). *Current English ordinance.* Department of Justice Bilingual Laws Information System. Retrieved from http://www.legislation.gov.hk/blis_ind.nsf/CurAllEngDoc/6DF192287B410B5248257309002E9CC2?OpenDocument

UNCTAD. (2016). *Review of maritime transport 2016*, UNCTAD/RMT/2016.

UNCTAD Secretariat. (1993). *Legal aspects of port management*, UNCTAD/SHIP/639.

U.S. House of Representatives. (2016). *United States code.* United States code. Retrieved from http://uscode.house.gov/

FSC
www.fsc.org
MIX
Papier | Fördert gute Waldnutzung
FSC® C083411

Kolibri 360 GmbH
Ferdinand-Jühlke-Straße 7
99095 Erfurt, Deutschland
produktsicherheit@kolibri360.de